Edward Staats de Grote Tompkins

Through David's Realm

Edward Staats de Grote Tompkins

Through David's Realm

ISBN/EAN: 9783337337278

Printed in Europe, USA, Canada, Australia, Japan

Cover: Foto ©Thomas Meinert / pixelio.de

More available books at **www.hansebooks.com**

THROUGH DAVID'S REALM

BY

EDWARD STAATS DEGROTE TOMPKINS

WITH TWO HUNDRED ILLUSTRATIONS
BY THE AUTHOR

TROY, N. Y
NIMS & KNIGHT
1889

To offer the public another book upon so trite a subject as the Holy Land may seem superfluous. Every view has been taken, from the serious and heavy volume of the conscientious scholar to the light and trivial book of humor. Only one excuse can be made for so great a presumption as this, and that is, although so much has been written, so little accurately describes the writer's own feelings and experiences. Perhaps the most interesting part of a book of travel is that which deals with commonplace every-day occurrences. The little discomforts, the hourly vexations, the cross-grained companions give the real interest, while description of places are read more eagerly when the atmosphere of personality surrounds them. Therefore I crave the reader's indulgence in attempting to lay before him an account, which shall be nothing learned, nothing ultra-serious, but calm, dispassionate, interspersed, perhaps, by the changes of an experience in a country where the solemn and the gay are somewhat incongruously intermingled. In short, I aim to tell the truth; to write as I felt, and not to gloss over difficulties or to lessen trials; to give unbiased accounts of what I saw, without respect to established authority or that kind of unwritten law which requires us to see in some things that which does not exist, and in others to close our eyes to that which is perfectly apparent. If I have written a stupid book, I shall have failed. If I should by chance succeed in interesting the reader, I shall have accomplished my desire.

With these few words I am willing to place the book in your hands, dear reader, asking only that I may be judged by what I attempt, and not by what some learned pedant may fancy I ought to have undertaken.

E. S. DeG. T.

CONTENTS.

XVIII.

Landing at Jaffa.

ONE Sunday morning I awoke and found the ship, in which we had sailed from Port Said, had come to rest. What could it mean? There was only one answer, we had arrived off Jaffa. The haste in which my toilet was made bore evidence to my eagerness to catch the first glimpse of the Holy Land. And yet I went on deck with a certain feeling that it could not be true; that this was some other place; and when my eyes looked out upon the scene before me, my heart almost stopped, for it seemed like some fair dream. For about one mile from the vessel was a pile of houses, which rose one above the other in picturesque fashion, gray and yellow in the early morning sun, while to the north and to the south stretched out

1

the sand banks, which ages of ceaseless beating of
the waves had cast up along the shore. Above
were the soft tints of the olive, and groves of the
orange tree. The rocks, which lay between us and
the shore, just showed their flat surfaces above the
water, while over the quiet blue level came hurrying
a crowd of boats each eager to be the first to touch
the vessel. The morning sunlight came softly
down, almost as it will through some haze, with
nothing but the scurrying boats to show this was
more than some picture, which superhuman skill
had painted. I pressed my eyes to make sure I was
not dreaming, while all the time the boats came
nearer, and just now, right under the side of the
huge black ship they bang against us as though we
had no feeling. Then, come yells and hoarse cries
in an unknown tongue, men fighting and scrambling
to see who shall be the first to mount the steps
which these eastern ships always carry. The peaceful Sabbath rest, which pervaded all the air, as was
fitting since this was our first visit to holy ground,
was doubtless startled by this savage attack, and fled
at the first appearance of the merciless Arabs of
Jaffa. The ship soon became the scene of an eager
pushing crowd, yet we remained quiet and content,
for were we not under powerful protection, even
that of Messrs. Cook and Son of London, who undertake all difficulties and all dangers, that they
may profit largely from the unwary and inexperi-

enced traveler. We knew that in good time all would be well, for somewhere there was a man who was bound to take care of us. Thus we were enabled to enjoy this confusion, this scrambling and noise.

At last a nice-looking man came off in a boat and mounted to the deck. He came at once to us, as though there was some invisible stamp by which members of a Cook's party can be identified. I looked to see if they had tied a label on me while I was unaware, but found none. It must have been the humility, the ignorance on our countenances, or perhaps it was the look of rest and supreme satisfaction which comes from a fancied security. We were soon picked out, our luggage put aboard a long-boat, and we were silently marshaled into another. Peacefully the boat glided over the smooth sea, and quietly it came up to the rock which served as a dock.

After landing we found ourselves in a new element of oriental life. Cairo had been tolerably clean, out of respect to the foreign population. But Jaffa, which does not cater to such popularity, is quite oriental in the sense that all refuse is thrown underfoot. The street runs along the water for a short distance, and is not over fifteen feet in its widest part. In it are camels, donkeys, men, women, and especially children. An occasional dog is seen, and everywhere the street is filled with rubbish and filth.

Jaffa does not look so nice when near at hand.   Indeed, few things do.   But then we came for all this,
and it is interesting after one gets over the first dis-

position to complain.   It was easy to
walk to the gate of the town, where we
passed through the portal and found carriages waiting to convey us to the hotel,
which is not in the city itself, but in a
suburb, built some years ago by German
settlers.   The road is lined with orange
trees covered with foliage and fruit, and
no picture could have been prettier than
this, now that humanity, that curse of
the East, is left behind and forgotten.

The hotel is quiet, homelike, and
almost European in its aspect.   The
rooms are small and cramped, I might
add ugly.   The landlord, a German,
welcomed us at the door, and we entered with
satisfaction, for the American flag waved over
our heads.   In the rear of the house were gardens
and trees, and we immediately began to investigate, but found nothing but commonplace things.
However, over the wall were beautiful orange
trees, laden with delicious fruit.   Our breakfast was
served at once, and it seemed strange to see the
American Consul passing us our plates.   But he did
it with a skill which showed he was fitted for the
occupation.   As he happened to be a German who

had never seen our shores, I readily forgave the apparent disrespect to our free and noble land.

But we soon issued from the inclosure of the house, and wandered out to find something to remind us of the many important episodes of history which gather about this place. To-day Jaffa seems but a collection of stone houses, more or less dilapidated, which rise one above another on the slight eminence on which it is built, until from the sea the city seems a succession of terraces. Around are beautiful gardens, making it indeed a perfect paradise, so long as one does not penetrate too far into the interior of the town. One can wander along the highways and dream of Peter and the house of Simon the Tanner, but if he dare to visit it he will dream no longer. Although the house may be rightly identified, it is so shabby

and dirty that one finds it difficult to fancy that on this terrace Peter had his celebrated vision. But we can roam around the outside and think of Hiram

who sent hither the cedars of Lebanon, of Jonah who
made the sea voyage, which ended in his going to
Nineveh against his will.   Or shall we reflect how
the Maccabeans attacked the town and destroyed
the shipping, or how it passed from Pompey to
Herod, and from Herod down through the ages,
witnessing the landing of the crusaders, alternately
demolished by pirates and rebuilt by the Romans?
Then there was the struggle between the Paynims
and the Christians, who successively took and re-
took it.   Here it was that Napoleon ordered the five
hundred soldiers in the hospital to be poisoned when
he was obliged to retreat.   And so it has gone from
one to another, as man has desired the position
which it afforded for the accomplishment of his own
selfish ends.

Its name is variously derived, but if the meaning
of Yafeh is the right one, that is "the beautiful,"
we need go no farther.   For there is somehow a
strange truth about this appellation, since as the
view from the windows of the hotel struck my vision
every artistic nerve rebounded ; for what fairy land
could equal this?   Far away through a soft haze
which obscured nothing, yet made everything exquisitely beautiful, stretched the blue Mediterranean.
The ships were riding at anchor just off the land,
while the lazy roll of the sea came slowly in to
shore.   Then we could see the soft sand with its
pale yellow and browns, making a pretty contrast

with the blue of the water. Jaffa was just far enough off to be picturesque, while the stains of time seemed but the marvelous skill of some far-famed colorist. As a foreground, right by our window, were the dark green orange trees with their fruit, whose reddish, golden gleams showed the richness beneath. All was quiet and silent, even the air and the sunlight apparently bowing in defer-

ence to our Sabbath day, and producing that infinite quiet which the soul demands at times, and especially finds when in communion with holy nature. Is there any delight in passing along path after path, only to have the peace disturbed by some rude Arab, whose sense of the fitting is in inverse ratio to the beauty of his surroundings? No, it is much better to see from afar and let those whose sense of rest is not so great, not so delicious, seek for the curiosities with a true Cockney spirit.

In the afternoon we set out to find the English
mission, which has been established here for some
time. We passed through those luxuriant groves of
orange trees of which I have spoken, and came at
last to the square, solidly built structures which ac-
commodate the children of the school and the rec-
tor of the mission. A large house, with a hall running through the middle and large rooms at the
side, formed a genuine English home. The missionary was a slight, pale, hard-worked man, whose wife
was even more attenuated than himself. They were
greatly disturbed at this time over the scandal caused
by a converted Jew, who had incurred a debt of
nearly three thousand dollars, in an imprudent manner, which the missionary society found themselves
obliged to pay, if they wished to accomplish any
work in that region. As it was, it had greatly hin-
dered whatever progress the cause was making.
This man had been stationed before on the coast of
Africa, where he had fallen into the same error. I
cannot understand the reasoning which prompted
such leniency on the part of the society.

A service was held in the chapel, where Dr. Cun-
ningham Geikie, one of our party, preached, which
was attended by the teachers of the schools and
some of the children. I could not see that there
was either great devotion or numerous attendance.

II.

The Road to Jerusalem.

MONDAY morning while we were at breakfast, the agent of Cook & Son came to each one of us, and asked whether we would prefer to go up to Jerusalem by carriage or on horseback. We nearly all replied "on horseback." We continued our meal, made dignified by the presence of the American Consul, when the agent came around to each one of us again and asked if we would as a personal favor go up in the carriages.

We were not disposed to be disagreeable, so consented, although we had been promised our choice, but in such a little thing we thought it would be unkind to be obstinate. Then we gathered our luggage together and consigned it to the dragoman, to whom we were now introduced. He was an American, with a deep red and brown complexion, caused by constant exposure to the wind and sun of the East. He was one of the unfortunate people who came out from Maine in 1866, under the excitement raised then by the Second Adventists, and who, thinking the world was coming to an end, desired to be on holy soil. The colony soon broke up and the members suffered a good deal. The Quaker City, when it visited Jaffa, took away those who remained at that time to Egypt, where they found some way of returning to their own country. But this young man, who had left home when he was eight, had remained in the country, and was now doing duty as dragoman whenever he could get employment.

At last it was settled how we should go, and we took our places in the landaus which Mr. Cook had had built in Switzerland, and drove away from the hotel over to the entrance of the highway leading up to Jerusalem. A more beautiful morning could not be imagined, as we passed through the charming fresh green trees and cactus hedges, into the plain. But just before we reached it, we saw a tomb with a graceful arch over it, whose white walls presented against the dark green of the foliage around, a pleasing picture. Some dragomans point it out as the tomb of Dorcas, but entirely without reason. From this we passed into the open country, and find ourselves in the Plain of Sharon. What memories arise as we are told that this is the plain so celebrated of old, although scholars refute the statement. The rose of Sharon, "Can we see one?" we next eagerly ask, and then a moment's thought shows us that the rose of Sharon is a question yet to be settled. But we do not mind, for if the rose of Sharon is not there we have the plain, plowed earth, the far-away distance as it stretches off toward the north or to the south in undulating waves. The country seems flat for the hills of Judea are far away behind much shrubbery, which hides them from view, while the rolling of the plain gives occasionally no view at all, and then one quite extended. The road is the pathway of ages, for along this track everything has gone up to Jerusalem, and if 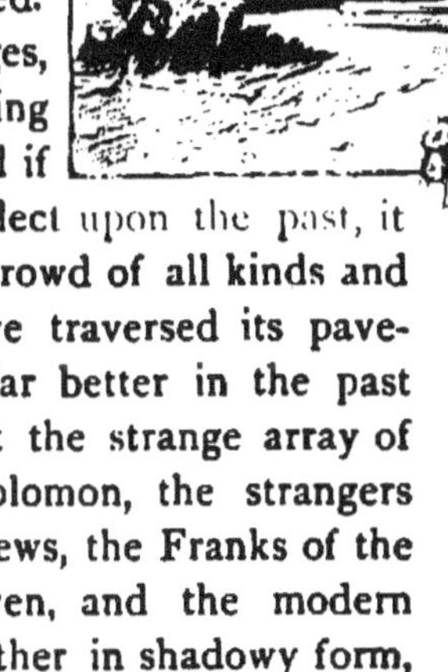 the mind is permitted to reflect upon the past, it will be filled with a motley crowd of all kinds and conditions of men, who have traversed its pavement, which was, we trust, far better in the past than it is in the present. But the strange array of warriors, the workmen of Solomon, the strangers from Tyre, the Romans, the Jews, the Franks of the middle ages, the Greeks even, and the modern French, all hustle along together in shadowy form, making the earth replete with history, crying out with outrage and crime, and seldom rejoicing with peace and happiness.

Yet the soil is fertile, the view is picturesque, the climate delicious, and all through the ages man has never ceased to oppress in some fashion this quarter of the globe. Even under the wise Solomon we

have the assurance that his power was tyrannical. E v e n when the crusaders sought to liberate the Holy S e p u l c h e r there was rapine and plunder, murder and crime. But this sunny March morning nothing could be more peaceful than the scene before us. Like all restless natures, the earth here has seemed disposed at last to take a rest. Even the natives are few, and the ground has been plowed, perhaps already sown with grain, and the people are patiently waiting for the increase.

The journey to Jerusalem is only forty miles long and can easily be made in one day ; but for convenience it is generally broken at Ramleh, a distance of twelve miles from Jaffa. Thus it seemed all too short when we found ourselves again entering gardens and orange groves, and perceived the road lined by the prickly pear. We soon drew up before the hotel, kept by a German, and until recently in a native building. But now modern enterprise has erected a building on the most conventional plan, one which might readily be found in any American village. I must say it grieved me to see in the midst of what was to me a highly picturesque place a building so out of harmony with its surroundings. But then it was comfortable and clean, and most people would for these reasons be grateful for its shelter. Our rooms were assigned, and we soon found that the midday meal was awaiting us. Afterward we entered the carriages to ride to Lydda, a town about four miles distant.

Lydda is one of the ancient cities of Palestine, and to-day presents the same features which all cities or villages do in this country ; the same narrow streets, extremely dirty, with children and men lounging about. The principal thing to see is the large church, which was built by Justinian and several times destroyed and rebuilt. It is a handsome building, and devoted to the Greek service. After a stroll through the bazaars we turned back toward Ramleh, the gentlemen preferring to walk as the road was so

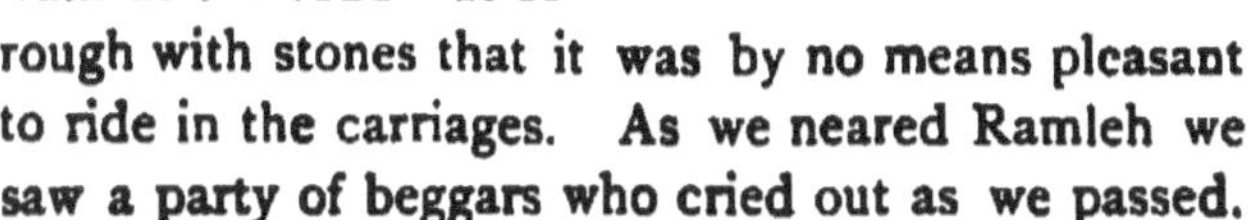

rough with stones that it was by no means pleasant to ride in the carriages. As we neared Ramleh we saw a party of beggars who cried out as we passed.

At first I paid but little heed to them until some one said they were lepers, and then we were all attention, as they were the first we had seen.

Nothing can exceed the loathsomeness which the leper inspires. However, at first sight, one does not fully comprehend how offensive they are. The face, a deep pink, which at first seems but the natural color, but which a second glance shows to be mixed with an ashen gray, appears very ghastly, as one reflects that it is the result of disease. Then, too, the disease appears in the form of great blotches, and these sometimes cover the whole cheek. But when one sees the fingers gone, and perhaps the hand dropped off, and the stump of the arm covered by this ashy pink blotch, then one realizes the loathsomeness of these poor creatures, who live by the charity of others. It is a mistake to think that leprosy is contagious as we generally suppose. It is to be contracted only after long dwelling in the places inhabited by these wretched people.

Fortunately, we soon left them behind, for they retired by the dragoman's orders, and we entered Ramleh, again passing through the high cactus hedges which line every highway near a town. Ramleh is a town of considerable size, with four thousand inhabitants, of whom nearly a third are Christians. Tradition, which is, however, very unreliable, says that Ramleh corresponds with Arimathea, and that here dwelt the Joseph who gave the ground for our Lord's burial.

There is a great tower of the old church built by the crusaders remaining here. Some authorities state that the architecture is clearly Saracenic, although it seems not unlike the early Norman style to be found in the north of France. A flight of one hundred and twenty steps leads to the top, where a most beautiful and extended view is to be obtained ; the whole Plain of Sharon from the hills of Judea to the sea, and from Carmel on the north to the sand plain of Philistia on the south, is stretched out before you ; Ashdod, Askelon and Gath, Gaza to the south, and Cæsarea to the north, the blue Mediterranean and the amber mountains on the east. The view is too full, and suggests too much. The eye gazes almost stupidly into the distance, where quiet reigns supreme, and

it takes another glance at the gardens beneath, with all their wealth of foliage and fruit, to convince one that this is a scene of earth. For otherwise, it might seem as if some fair god had drawn over the mind a magic spell, which opened up at once the

place and the history, the charm and the reality,
where all the world has met, incited by rage or
moved with religious feeling. Yet, how peaceful it
lies before the eye, stretching out on every side in
hazy rest, as though the long storm being past there
was indeed a cessation from its labors, a haven even
for this troubled soil, and in its old age a sense of
quiet, which must come to all stormy natures
after a life which has nourished and fed many
people.

For, although we think of the Philistines of ancient memory, or of the Children of Israel fighting
for the happy land, or whether we fancy that yon
bluish amber hills to the east are hiding gems of
beauty for us to seize, or whether we look over the
vast blue sea toward our own sweet land, we must,
upon this entrance to this sacred country, bow before that Almighty Will which has so surely brought
order out of chaos, and rest from strife, and happiness from misery. It needs no skeptic hand to
point out the errors of men, they are all too plain
before us. But it also needs no apology to prove
that God is Lord of all. If history condensed into
one small space can bear a proof, we have it here.
Before us lies a scene which has been the center of
all the earth. And if a hazy cloud intercepts the
hills, among which our Lord has wandered, and if
the north is out of sight, we know it is not far away,
and that we are standing at the threshold of a new

life, for are we not entering that most holy of all places, the place where our Lord has lived ?

And while the eye can range around this scene, and the retina be dazzled with a lustrous beauty, there must be a certain undefined longing toward those hills afar off, and yet much nearer than we think. But that will come to-morrow. For the present we must leave with a sigh this vision of beauty—for it is beautiful—and turn our attention to the convent below us. It was formerly, until the enterprise of Mr. Cook provided a hotel, the only place where man could get a lodging between Jaffa and Jerusalem. And I for one must express my regret that Mr. Cook ever lived. I felt this even more strongly after I had entered its cool, vault-like rooms, with their white beds and their air of mystery. To remain in this place, at least would be a romance, while where we were we were so very comfortable that I never gave my surroundings a thought after the sun went down.

These hours in Ramleh, the first taste of the Holy Land, still linger in my memory as the pleasantest I have ever spent. Would that one could always have such peace, such happiness, such quiet ! And yet we could not drive the world quite away, for there was Mr. Cook's agent with us all the time, a bustling, handsome American, who was intent upon destroying our peace of mind by his unromantic ways. Then, too, as the western sun was sinking slowly, yet as it seemed regretfully, because there

2

was in my heart a desire that it should remain, and when the Judean hills were coming out in bolder relief against the pinkish sky, up drove my old companions, whom I had left in Cairo, as I supposed, forever. It was an inundation of the States in good earnest. The hotel was full because we were an especial Cook's party and took the best. At once there was quarreling and bickering about accommodations. The spell was gone. I surrendered at last. The sun might go down, and the Judean hills might fade, I cared not ; I was now in America, the most unromantic and commonplace country on the globe. No sooner had the first carriage come up, than I heard at once a wail. What was it ?

" Papa is furious," cried the young ladies.

" At what ? " I asked recklessly, for I did not wish to be disturbed.

" He will tell you," and then up dashed the other carriage. I saw wrath on all their faces. I was not to blame, and I could not understand why I must receive the first explosion of anger, just because I happened to be a friend of theirs. But such is the fate of friends. It was all the fault of the agent. What could it be? I soon found out after hearing three stories at once. The agent had simply deceived them.

" That's nothing," I remarked phlegmatically, " for a man who travels or stays at home must get accustomed to that after a time."

" But," cried the western merchant, " he said we should all have landaus, and look at that thing."

" What is the matter with it ? " I asked, innocently, gazing at a very respectable wagon which was, it is true, not a landau.

" Can't you see ?" demanded the merchant, angrily.

" Yes," I replied, amused, " but I am not to blame."

" Who said you were ? "

" No one said so, but you rather infer it by your manner," I answered.

" I am angry with that agent.   He is a perfect scamp."

" I do not doubt it," I replied.

It seems that it was a clear case of misrepresentation.   It was our first experience with the agents of Cook, and it was not, alas ! the last.

We entered our carriages the next morning, having passed a good night, although I, who seemed fated to share the troubles of the whole party, was amused, and at the same time a little wearied to hear the Reverend Doctor from New York abuse the dragoman in language not generally thought appropriate out of a pulpit.   But this only amused, after I had forgotten the disgust, and we started out from Ramleh with pleasant expectations.   On every side were suggestions of the Bible ; first a man plowing, and then the land-marks consisting of heaps of stones.   After about an hour's ride we came to the Valley of Ajalon, and one must look with curiosity upon this place, so remarkable for the command of Joshua, who directed the sun and the moon to stand still, while he thus gained time to slaughter the Canaanites. Away to the left we passed the ancient Gimzo, which was taken from the Israelites in the time of Ahab. This was bringing the Bible very near home, and one can hardly realize that those stories we all know so well are true, and that this pile of houses, half built, is the real site of an ancient city. Then we come to Gezer, where Joshua defeated its king and gave it to the Kohite Levites. But it was not dispossessed of its original inhabitants, and long remained a stronghold of the Philistines. David besieged it, and afterward Pharaoh took and destroyed it, and Solomon rebuilt it. Then we have near us Makkedah, the cave where Joshua shut up the five kings of the Amorites until he had defeated their armies.

We were now ascending the low hills which extend out into the plain, leaving behind the view which we had of the sea, and only catching glimpses thereof as we find ourselves on some prominent point of land. Vegetation is beginning to disappear, only showing itself in the valleys, while the hills are covered with a reddish earth which seems to produce nothing. We now come to the village of Latrûn, or " the robber," where tradition says that the two thieves met the Holy Family when they were going down to Egypt, and one of them, who afterward threw himself upon the mercy of our Lord when on the cross, protected the Divine Infant from the brutality of his comrade. The places along the route have some historical connection, but it would be too wearisome to mention them all. The carriages arrived at a place called Bab-el-Wady, or in English, the "entrance to the valley." Here there is an inn kept by a Jew. It was of great

interest to us because in it we took our first meal from native hands. As it is characteristic of the country, I will describe it.

Like all buildings in this part of Palestine it is entirely built of stone, because of the scarcity of timber. The first floor is a stable which has all the appearance of a dungeon, being entered by an archway, and receiving its light from it. On either hand is a flight of stone steps leading up to an open court-yard, or platform, around which are situated the rooms belonging to the inn. One side is a large parlor, while the other two sides are occupied with bedrooms and kitchen. All the rooms are arched, and present a very strange yet comfortable appearance. The stone was white, well cleaned, although I judge the inn has not always borne such a reputation. Our luncheon was laid out in a long parlor, and we sat down to a very comfortable and bountiful meal. Peace had been restored to the discordant elements of the party, and as Mr. Cook's agent had ridden on ahead so as to reach Jerusalem before us, I was quite restored to favor by my quondam friends. After dinner, sufficient time was allowed for me to make a hasty sketch, and then we resumed our ride, which began to grow a little wearisome as the horses toiled up the mountains. However, at the top of the first mountain, we obtained a splendid view of the sea and the plain below. We paused

awhile to take our last look, and then turned our faces steadfastly toward Jerusalem.

As we progressed the hills became more and more barren, until we thought they could become no worse. Yet, as we passed along, we found that still greater desolation was in store for us, for the valleys themselves looked barren and poor, and all became brown earth without the semblance of fer-

tility. When we came to Abou Gosch, a place rendered famous in recent times as the dwelling of a
noted robber, our thoughts were turned backward
into the past, and we thought of the Ark of God,
which rested at Kir-jath-jearim, waiting twenty
years for the Children of Israel to bring it unto
Jerusalem.

So we passed on from one place to another, each
miserable and small, sometimes consisting of very
few houses, but each rich in past associations, each
one bringing up some point which gave the mind a
series of pictures, since here was fought that struggle
which lasted through so many years, the quarrel
between the Children of Israel and their formidable
enemies, the Philistines. But I, longing to catch
some glimpse of Jerusalem, feel sure that the first
impression that the dragoman had of me was, that
I was unusually inquisitive. For, every half hour I
would ask if nothing was yet to be seen of the Holy
City, and he would answer, "no." Then I begged
him to tell me when the first sight could be obtained,
for I, like all people who have never been there,
supposed it was a city set on a hill, and that from the
distance the holy place would stand aloft like some
beacon-light. However, we went up hill and down
through valleys, all more or less interesting, but each
giving, by its poverty-stricken appearance, a kind
of monotony, until, as we really approached the city,
the tops of the hills were seamed with the torrents

of ages, as all the soil had been washed down into the valleys ; then, on-coming torrents would sweep away what was in the valleys until they became desolate, too. When these hills were covered with a dense forest, and the valleys were filled with vines and fig-trees, and sometimes the hillsides were terraced, a scene of great richness must have been presented. Indeed, one can easily picture this richness, for still there remain the ruins of terraces. But the desolation of the land now is all apparent. For truly the curse of the Lord seems to have been poured out literally upon these hills, and to have run down their sides in streaks. Nothing but a feeling of profound sadness can come to one reflecting how this ruin was caused, how the curse of the Lord was brought upon this willful and miserable race. No tale of retribution can so completely cut to the heart as this. It is not the result of one sin, but of repeated sin, repeated obstinacy ; and now the marauding Arab holds possession, while the children of the soil are in other lands, a wandering people. If one had tears to weep they should shed them now. For what greater crime can history show than that which has stripped one of the fairest lands on earth, until it is now the most desolate.

Perhaps a skeptic hand can point where lies the fallacy of such an argument, but it seems to me that hostile criticism must acknowledge that truly the prophecy of God's servants and of God's Son has been terribly and truly fulfilled.

But after going rapidly down a steep hill we have Kolonieh pointed out, the place which is supposed to be the Emmaus of St. Luke's gospel. Here we see a few signs of fertility, for there are orchards and gardens set down in a valley, which, from its situation, ought to be very beautiful. Crossing a bridge the carriage stops, and we descend to pick up stones from the brook, for here they say David took the five smooth stones which he used to kill the giant Goliath. From here to Jerusalem it is a ride of about an hour and a half, and all the way up hill. But I did not know that, and so repeated my inquiries of the driver. The last hour was tiresome, for there was nothing but the expectation of the Holy City, and this seemed to withhold itself from view in the most obstinate manner. At last, however, the carriage began to descend, we passed some houses, and before we realized that we were surrounded by habitations, the carriage stopped and the dragoman told us to dismount. It was like some dream, difficult to comprehend, for we were at the Jaffa Gate and this was Jerusalem. What jugglery was this? We had been coming down a hill and Jerusalem lay below us. But there stands the gateway before us, with its dark gray stones, somehow insignificant, yet as we looked at it quite natural. There was nothing to do but to accept the situation as best we might, but I felt that I had been cheated out of that first sight of the city, for I thought if it were placed on a hill and surrounded by hills we must first see it, then go down into the valley, and then up.   But to come upon it as a bird might, simply to light down, without any valley, so confused me that I walked through the gate and to the hotel which adjoins in a manner perfectly dazed.

III.

Points of Interest.

OUR first impulse was most natural, to seek the roof of the hotel and gain a view of this wonderful city itself.   We lost no time, but soon found ourselves panting and out of breath on the top of the house, whence a splendid view of the whole city and the surrounding country could be obtained.   Of course, as soon as I had this vantage ground I saw at once where had been my mistake.   Instead of being placed on a hill with other hills around it, Jerusalem is placed upon the slope of a hill, on two sides of which deep valleys cut into the earth, leaving one corner, that on which the Temple stood, high in air.   These two valleys join at this corner, and form a wady running all the way to the Dead Sea, so that from the roof of the hotel it was quite possible to see down through this cut across the Dead Sea to the land of Moab.

Then the Temple corner, which had always, somehow, seemed to my excited imagination to tower up above all the rest of the city, standing out in great prominence, is actually the lowest part of the whole town. The only way in which it could have been conspicuous from the rest of the city is, that with this for a center, the rest of the houses may be said to rise in a semicircle around it, so that from the top of each house the Temple would be clearly visible. However, as we stood on the roof of the hotel and looked off, it took some time to accustom ourselves to the fact that yon low elevation was the Mount of Olives. It seemed so near, almost within one's grasp. And then the Mosque of Omar, which was, as it seemed, directly under us, appeared almost insignificant. David's hill, Mount Zion, was just at our right, while only a stone's throw off was the Church of the Holy Sepulcher. The Pool of Hezekiah was beneath us, and where I stood one could look down into the water.

It all seemed so strange, so very strange, as the sun was getting a little pale in the western sky, to see the deepening night dropping its pall over the soft, gray city below us. The quiet of the hour added to the weird grayness of the scene, and as we watched, it seemed as if some picture made by hand had been before our vision and now was slowly fading away, so as to make room for another. Yet Olivet remained clear before us, and the top of Omar caught the few last gleams of the sun, while deep, thick night gathered fast in the narrow streets around, threatening soon to envelop us too. But then, when the light had faded from Omar's picturesque dome, and Olivet, sadly it seemed, plunged under the coverlid of gloom, we turned as one released from a dream to think of our surroundings. While still the light was with us it was all too strange, and this could not be the Jerusalem we had read of, the Jerusalem we loved, for it was all too commonplace, all too much of earth. But night advancing brought out its own bright torches, as if in pity to see us waiting there without any light, and slowly we could discern a building here and an outline there, until from out of the vagueness grew up the mystic city, the city of David, the city we loved. Faint and beautiful like some. dear friend it rose before us, and in the deepening gloom we could hear our Savior's voice, we could see the shadowy forms of His Disciples, the crowds with bated breath, the poor, the sick, all hushed in deference to his great wisdom, which alone could speak. And it was that simple truth, so great in its power, so wonderful in its might, which spoke to us now.

"Come unto me all ye that labor and are heavy laden." Were ever words better fitted for a weary traveler, or was there ever a more soothing sense of rest than this which now stole over me as I stood there in the very center of his work? a center, alas! where few believe in Him or follow in His footsteps. If the Christian can ever feel a sense of restfulness in the arms of his Lord he must feel it three-fold more when he is treading the very ground which his Lord has trod.

Out from the dimness spoke so many spirits that with this crowd of shadowy forms came others, until all the place seemed crowded, until all seemed gathered around one man, seeking to hear again those words of wisdom which have been so long rejected; the prophets of old, David with his warriors, Solomon with his magnificence, the princes of Judah with their abominations, the armies of the great Assyrian kings, the Chaldees, the Romans, and then our Lord, a poor man who had not where to lay his Head, standing far above them all, standing out among men, a hero even if He were not a God! Alas! what is earthly fame, what is glory, what is ambition? These walls so many times rebuilt, so many times destroyed, this city which has been so oft a heap of stones, is but positive proof of the weakness of man and the power of God. It needs no stronger sermon than these stones to turn men from their evil deeds.

So before me in the darkness there seems to loom

up a great and wonderful city, for it is the city of the dead. The spirits of those who have gone before are filling the Valleys of Jehoshaphat and Hinnom, while all the streets are thronged to their fullest extent. The house-tops are black, it is with people, and far out on Mount Olivet there stands another crowd, so dense no man can number them ; and so to the north, and far out from the Damascus Gate they stand, these people who have gone before and people with their presence these silent streets of to-day. Yet all goes on the same, a dragoman comes stamping into the hotel below, the feeble lights of the houses begin to appear ; and slowly, sadly, the multitude of those who have sinned and perished are fading away, and we are roused to the demands of an unfortunate and unsympathetic civilization. If we could leave Jerusalem with these impressions, with two pictures before the eyes, the real with strange beauty, or the imaginary with greater weirdness, we would be content. I was fain to hasten away and forget that I had seen the place itself. It were better to have the eye retain two images, and yet I was there to see it all, and to discover many things which pain a lover of the true and good.

I think the week I spent in Jerusalem was one of the happiest, if not the happiest I ever passed. Never can I remember a week spent with such purity of aim and such exaltation of sentiment, and yet even that state of mind was rudely and violently upset by the untoward circumstances by which I was surrounded. But even the things which annoyed could not deprive me of that sense of blessed privilege which I had in treading the same ground, seeing the same scene, and thinking the same thoughts our Savior thought.

In visiting Jerusalem one cannot but feel that the landmarks are extremely uncertain, and that he is obliged to take all statements with great reserve. There are but few things which are unquestioned. Of course, among these must be the Mount of Olives and the Valleys of Jehoshaphat and Hinnom. Even the site of the Temple is questioned, and many are willing to put it upon the Hill of Zion which rises to a considerable h e i g h t, and which would have given it a very stately position. But the country around

must exhibit something of the same general aspect, although we are of course aware that in the time of our Lord it was far more beautiful, and was covered with a rich and profuse vegetation. Now the appearance of Jerusalem is peculiarly a hill-town. It is among the mountains, and, although these mountains do not appear so very high, they do present all

3

the appearance of barrenness and roughness. Stones are protruding from the ground everywhere, and to our eyes, which have been so long accustomed to see fertile fields, and to consider stones significant of sterile soil, the appearance of all the country around Jerusalem is pitiably poor.   There is, indeed, in the ordinary acceptation of the term very little beauty to be found there.   It has all departed, like its people, some day we hope to return.   Many wonder how it can be possible that Judea should ever regain its former position as a flourishing country.   But they wonder because they have never carefully examined the causes of its present poverty.   In the first place we must remember that it was ever a poor country in point of natural advantages.   The hills were, perhaps, covered with trees and a certain amount of soil was there.   But it was the fortress of a rude king who sought only a stronghold.   After David's time, when the glory of Solomon brought around it so much wealth, the hills were terraced and the whole country cultivated to a high state of fertility.   And every one who knows says, that the power of this soil, as barren as it seems, is something marvelous.   Thus, with the care of a large population, a most beautiful landscape could be made. With the misfortune of centuries the trees have been cut down, and none planted in their place, the soil has been washed off from the hillsides, the terraces are all but gone, we can only see the traces left, and gradually the country has been stripped of its opportunity to regain its former state. But it only wants a good government, a careful system of agriculture, two hundred years of nursing, and these hills would bloom like the rose. Scientists admit this, and, doubtless, if the English Government would guarantee a safe and responsible government this resurrection would be going on now.

The saddest sight one can possibly see is fallen greatness. It does not much matter whether it be man or city, it is all the same, and I know of nothing more touching than those evidences which prove great opportunities, and which show such unutterable degradation. Jerusalem has just this aspect. It is a city which has repented in sackcloth and ashes, but a city which has not yet found forgiveness. Now it is degraded, like a person of noble opportunities, who has let one sin after another undermine the character, until the state of sin is so great and the hope of regeneration is so small, that utter despair seems the only end. Yet, we are promised that Jerusalem shall rise and one day resume its former glory.

It was with these things well in mind that I set

out to view the city more carefully. I found the streets dry and looked in vain for that filth for which it is famed. The place is not large, although it contains twenty thousand inhabitants. A half mile in either direction would be about the distance traversed in going from our hotel to the furthest gate. The Christian quarter is well built and comfortable. Large convents and churches, schools and dwellings line the narrow streets, and present only their small, barred windows to the passer-by. The Arab quarter shows less regard to regularity, and the bazaars especially are like most Eastern shops, very much dilapidated and shabby. There seemed nothing to buy, and there was no air of business, but a lazy stillness, a sort of dogged obstinacy, expressed in the faces of the natives as we went along.

The Church of the Holy Sepulcher is generally

the first object of attention, and as it was near to our hotel, we were not long in reaching it. Outside, it presents that rough appearance which is so characteristic of the East, while within it shows great gorgeousness of decoration. However, it seemed to be rather small, and especially is this the case when one tries to comprehend the number of sacred places which tradition endeavors to include within its walls. But as I am rather skeptical about such things, I simply wandered over the church to admire the ornamentation. The tomb itself is picturesque, but recent explorations have proven without doubt that it could not be the place where our Lord was buried. The different religious bodies have chapels within the church, and one wonders how they all manage to keep the peace. Indeed, they do not always succeed in so doing.

One cannot but reflect upon the massacre which took place there when Ibrahim Pasha was governor. Surely, to an unbeliever such religion must seem a farce. Then, too, all about the church are evidences of such gross superstition that a Moslem, who is certainly simple in his faith, must wonder why the intelligent Christian has so many erratic fancies. Perhaps the greatest drawback to Christianity in this country is the great diversity of belief as contrasted with the single line of thought in the Moslem creed.

The Sepulcher itself, although beautiful in design,

fails to impress one with its size or dignity.   I fancy it was conceived on too grand a scale for its proportions, for it gives one the idea that it was intended to be large.

The Mosque of Omar is thought by most scholars to stand in the same place where the Temple stood. To gain admission to the Temple inclosure, which occupies a fourth part of the city itself, one has to have the intervention of his consul. But as we were under the tutelage of Mr. Cook we were saved all this bother. When one has passed the gateway he finds a great open court, in the center of which stands the celebrated mosque. Indeed, one cannot say enough of its beauty, for it is the best preserved specimen of Arabic architecture which I have seen. Without it is covered with richly colored porcelain tiles, and the frieze is ornamented with texts from the Koran. There are four gates facing the points of the compass. The appearance from without is not so graceful as one might expect, but the exquisite coloring, as one gets near to it, makes it supremely beautiful. Within it is rather dark, as the light comes through the peculiar stained glass of the Arabs, which consists of a pattern made of clay and glass put in, in little pieces, something on the plan of a mosaic.

The result is undeniably rich and elegant, but the amount of light let in is very little. There are two rows of pillars, the inner one supporting the great dome which covers the rock. Over the whole there is an ex- quisitely beautiful coating of

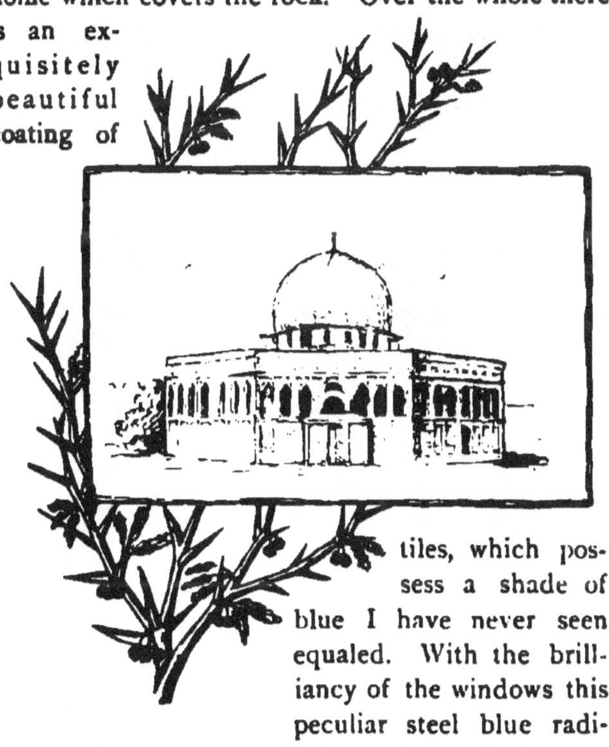

tiles, which pos- sess a shade of blue I have never seen equaled. With the brilliancy of the windows this peculiar steel blue radiance makes a scene of almost heavenly beauty. Under this dome the sacred rock appears in all its roughness.

It is here that Abraham is supposed to have

offered up his son Isaac. Here the Ark of the Covenant stood. On this rock is written the unutterable name of God which only Jesus can pronounce. The Mohammedans say that from here Mohammed ascended to heaven on his good steed El Burak, and that the rock wanted to follow him, but that Gabriel kept it down.

Just opposite the Mosque of Omar is that of El Aksa. But between them is a beautiful pulpit of Saracenic work with columns and arches, doubtless the remains of some elegant structure. The pavement is very good and the whole area is kept in better condition than one generally sees in mosques. At the side nearest the Mount of Olives is the Gate

Beautiful, now closed, but formerly the great and beautiful gate leading into the Temple. Without are two arches and within is an ornamentation which shows a corresponding arrangement.

It is a pleasant thing to lean over the wall and look down into the valley below, and it is with a feeling of awe as one does so, for even now the distance seems great, and we are told that in times past the valley was much deeper. It is only the feeling that here was the Temple of God that makes the place of paramount interest. Of itself there is little to see besides the beautiful Mosque of Omar. Olivet, however, rises on the other side of the valley, appearing more like the natural rise of ground than like a mountain famous for its historical associations.

In spite of the lassitude, the feeling of dreaminess, which is so natural to one visiting a place affording so much food for reflection as Jerusalem, there comes over one at last a certain desire to come into contact, if that be possible, with every work of antiquity. There exists to-day, fortunately, a few traces of the old city. While there is so much glaring fraud everywhere, here and there the scholars connected with the Palestinian Exploration Fund have brought to light many points of interest. Of course, their researches have not proved many things with positiveness, only with a certain degree of probability ; there still remains, however, the chance that we can come directly in contact with the old city.

One of the most disputed points is the shape and appearance of the city under the Romans. We learn from Josephus certain facts, which, instead of proving definitely anything, seem only, in the hands of contending parties, to obscure the truth. These statements are, of course, a basis, but instead of taking them as meaning anything more than a mere description, scholars, with the idea that the present site of the Holy Sepulcher is the true one, have distorted them into so many different shapes that poor old Josephus would stand aghast to see how he has been mangled. But then this faithful old Jew, even if he did make mistakes, would learn also, doubtless to his astonishment, were he alive to-day, that he is an atrocious liar. Alas ! it is the fate of all historians. Age, instead of giving dignity and adding veneration, seems only to add calumny. I do not myself doubt that Josephus was a conscientious old man who sought to tell the truth so far as it was consistent with the dignity of his nation, and more than this one cannot expect of any historian. Had he given exact facts, those detrimental as well as those which are complimentary, he would have been cried down as unpatriotic, a fault which is particularly heinous in a Jew.

So when Josephus makes some casual remark about the situation of his own city there are not wanting those who will make his plain words appear different from what he intended. Jerusalem, we learn, was first built on Mount Zion, which has always been a citadel or stronghold. Josephus mentions that it was surrounded by valleys, but until recently this seemed strange, for now there is very little indication of any valley within

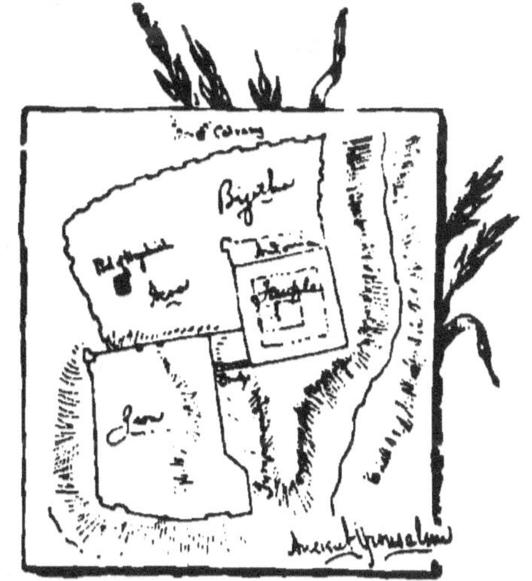

the walls. But a little thought directed into the proper channel shows, if Zion was a high hill with a wall all around it, and opposite was another hill, the two being separated by a ravine, that, when the walls and palace, which stood within them, were demol-

ished, the débris would naturally fill up the valley.
Such, indeed, was the case.   Exploration has shown
that a ravine does exist, filled up with the accumu-
lations of centuries.   This ravine ran from the Jaffa
Gate, or the Tower of David, which stands just
beside the Jaffa Gate, eastward until it touched the
Temple Hill or Mount Moriah, when it turned
nearly at right angles to the south.   If Zion were a
citadel, such a configuration would be perfectly
natural; for, of course, it would be separated from the
rest of the city by a wall.   Without a deep ditch or
ravine, the wall would, of course, be of little use.
To-day a deep cut around the Tower of David
proves that there was once some kind of a valley.
Measurements made recently show that the Tyropean, which is undoubtedly the same valley, was
thirty-three feet below the present surface, and that
toward the east it is twenty feet below the present
street of David.

So when the Mount of Zion is
once clearly placed we can then
visit the famous and well-known
Robinson's Arch.   The corner
of the Temple to the southwest
was nearly opposite to the
northeast corner of Mount
Zion. This bridge was, doubtless, a passage-way for
the king and court from the palace which stood on
Zion to the Temple.   Below, as one of the courts of

the palace, was the forum, or open place used by the public, which was called the Xistus.

To-day one stands before these huge stones, which are blackened and weather-stained beyond anything which I have ever seen, and recollects that here in all probability we have a part of Solomon's Temple. It is bringing those days very near. That these stones should have upheld his royal feet, that all the Jewish kings have passed over this spot, that in spite of such awful destruction as the city has passed through, these stones still remain, may well strike the beholder with awe. It requires but little imagination to picture this structure spanning the valley for the distance of three hundred and fifty feet. Its width was fifty feet, as is shown by the three courses of stones which project from the Temple wall. The foundations of the first pier were laid upon the rock forty-two feet below the spring of the arch. As the street is now nearly up to the arch, this gives some little idea, both of the débris which has been thrown in here, and also of the former depth of the valley below. There were five piers with spans of about forty feet each. Near one of the piers Captain Warren broke through the pavements and sunk a shaft to the rock twenty-three feet below. Here he found a drain cut into the rock twelve feet deep and four feet wide, connected with some remarkable cisterns. In his search he found remains of another bridge farther up the valley, which appeared still older, going back at least to the time of Solomon, if indeed the former did not. It is at any rate certain that the former bridge existed in the time of Herod, and no one knows how much earlier.

Passing along toward the north we come to a small inclosed court where are some stones supposed

to be of the ancient Temple. Their appearance is sufficiently ancient, and their beveled sides have seen many years of grief. For this is the Wailing Place of the Jews, where the bigotry of the Mohammedans allows them to come and weep over the destruction of their city. Travelers speak of the scene which takes place here every Friday as something infinitely touching. Indeed, were the wailing of such a nature that one could discover actual grief, it might be. My experience proved to me, that it was a sort of religious service, in which the poor, miserable Jews of Jerusalem indulged, partly perhaps because they had nothing else to do, and partly because the pity of travelers often moves them to put sums of money into the hands of those who look the most miserable and appear the most heart-broken. In short, the whole thing is a farce, and the sentimental feelings of people encourage what is to the Jew a very profitable grief.

Being somewhat skeptical about a grief which is over eighteen hundred years old I watched them while they were at their lamentations, and could discover nothing but a kind of mumbling, a droning which was attended by far more interest in the onlookers than in the place itself. Of course, the traveler can take a great interest in this wall, which shows so evidently the stamp of antiquity. In fact there is not much reason to doubt that it was part of the old Temple.

A little way beyond is the evidence of another arch discovered by Wilson. But modern investigation has decided that it could hardly have seen even the time of Herod.

The ancient Jerusalem was built upon three principal hills. Zion, Moriah, and that which Josephus calls Akra. Zion and Moriah were placed almost with their corners together, the one lapping over a little beyond the other. At this corner was the bridge already spoken of. Around the north of both these hills was built a third city, which rose up from the valley in a semicircular manner like an amphitheater. Indeed, Josephus speaks of the Temple being in the center, and Zion and Akra forming the semicircle around it. After the city became more prosperous, the suburbs of course greatly increased, extending far without the city wall beyond the Jaffa Gate. After a time this suburb was inclosed and the whole made one city. Then, too, there must have been other walls and fortifications without the walls which inclosed the city, for we read that the " outer wall was forced by the enemy giving them possession of the lower Tyropean valley."

At present we find Jerusalem for the most part level, that is, with none of the great divisions which existed in earlier times. The accumulation of all sorts of rubbish, the decline of the place as a fortress, and the general poverty of the country after the Roman destruction led to this end. So we have to-day a very imperfect representation of the city as it was when in its prime. The main features are of course the same ; we have the Valley of Jehoshaphat on one side, and the Valley of Hinnom on the other. These are localities which cannot be disputed. In Hinnom we see with considerable clearness the different places mentioned in the Bible. The place where the image of Moloch was set up by Solomon must be in the deep gorge at the bottom of the valley. The thought that here the awful sacrifices of children were made, that here the abominations against which the prophets spoke were carried on, is particularly thrilling. Especially is this the case if one has come from the Temple wall, where he is brought into direct contact with Solomon's Temple itself, with all its glorious memories. Farther up the valley we still see the pool of Gihon. To-day the valley seems pleasant and cheerful, for Cook has built here a large warehouse for his tents and luggage used in taking travelers through the country. Other enterprises have sprung up, and, as the valley is not far from the new Frank quarter, it is rapidly losing that air of desolateness which the Valley of Jehoshaphat still possesses.

We have still to visit the Tombs of the Kings, as they are called, but often known as the Tomb of Helena. Passing up from the Valley of Hinnom, we go by the buildings of the Russian Hospice into the open country, until we come to the road leading up to Damascus. Here we see paths leading in an indefinite manner across the fields, but the dragoman who is behind comes up and shows us the way. Descending a long flight of steps we find ourselves in a court nearly square. The walls are of a deep yellow, almost a brown, cut out of the natural rock. At one side is an archway also cut out of the rock and ornamented with a debased kind of Greek architecture. Entering the vestibule we perceive a narrow opening at the left, protected formerly by a door, which was so cleverly made as to be almost impossible to discover. Within was another door as a sort of trap by which to catch the unwary. From without it yielded easily to pressure, but when let go returned to its place and was then immovable from within.

The first room is about eighteen feet square, while from it open three other rooms somewhat smaller. From these the tombs extend by narrow, low openings into the rock on every side. Even beyond the tomb itself there is sometimes another chamber. In an under chamber, reached by a flight of steps, was found the sarcophagus, thought by M. de Saulcy to be that of David.

Modern research has shown pretty conclusively that these tombs could hardly have existed before the time of Herod, and some, indeed, contend that they were much later. There is such evidence to

show that Helena, the queen of Monobazus, king of
Adiabene, built them, that it is now generally accepted as a fact.

Beyond the Tombs of the Kings are those of the
Judges. They are similar in character, and a visit
to one of them is sufficient to establish an idea of
ancient Jewish tombs. An ancient tomb has been
recently discovered near the northern wall of the
city not far from the Damascus Gate, which Mr. ()li-
phant thinks may possibly be the real Holy Sepulcher. He says it might as well be this
as any other. True, but it is quite as
easy to say, it might as well have been
another as this. The remains of an
ancient church were recently uncovered, built by the Empress Eudoxia,
to the memory of St. Stephen, on the
spot where he was martyred. This would set at rest
any question about the public place of execution,
and thus bring out clearly the fact that the Holy
Sepulcher must be within a short distance from this
spot.

The subject is one which has agitated people so
much during the last few years that it seems almost
unnecessary to discuss it here. Mr. Prime under-
takes in his " Tent Life " to prove that the Church
of the Holy Sepulcher must be the place. The first
glance which I gave the city proved to me beyond a
doubt that it could not be the true site. We know

positively that Jerusalem during the time of our Lord was large and populous. To-day it has only about twenty thousand inhabitants, and the Church of the Holy Sepulcher stands quite within the walls. The contour of the hills is such that if the wall of the city be made to pass within the Holy Sepulcher the city would assume a very singular shape. Indeed, all the arguments which Mr. Prime adduces are quite out of the question. If the city is to be considered as containing one hundred thousand inhabitants, it must cover far more ground than it does at present. It can extend over the rest of Mount Zion and stretch out beyond the Jaffa Gate. In this way the matter could have been accomplished. But if it is to be cut off from the direction to the northwest, it must remain a small city of necessity. Thus we must go beyond the present walls, at least, to find a solution for our difficulty.

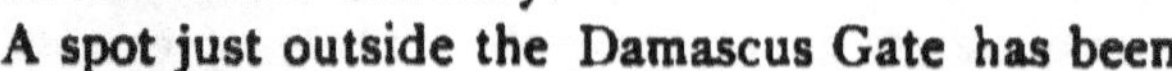

A spot just outside the Damascus Gate has been agreed upon as the most probable place. Indeed, it seems strange to me that this spot has not been chosen before, for it was the place which Jewish tradition has always assigned as the place of execution. Of this there seems to be little doubt. If, then, there was a place which was known to be used for this purpose, why have the scholars been so long in finding it out ?   Why was it not assumed that the same spot would be chosen for the crucifixion of our Lord ?   Indeed, when I was in Jerusalem as late as that, no guide-book could be found which spoke of this hill as the true Calvary.

The late General Gordon had a theory about the place which is rather more novel than valuable. He assumes this to be the place of the skull.   Indeed, when we reached the spot, going around the walls outside of the city, we found that it had a certain appearance of the top of a man's head.   General Gordon assumed, as this was the skull, that the rest of the body was to be found.   The chest he took to be the quarries which lie below the hill, and from which it is extremely probable the stone was taken to build the Temple.   From this he arrived at his emblematic character of the city as signifying in actual configuration the New Jerusalem.   An early tradition makes this the place of the stoning of St. Stephen.   Indeed, there is no doubt about its being the regular place of crucifixion.   The tract has always been considered unlucky, another proof of its original character.

A very interesting discovery recently made of a tomb, supposed to be that of Joseph of Arimathea, has led opinion more strongly in this direction. The fact that ten years after the Crucifixion Agrippa built large towers on this spot accounts for the true

Calvary being lost sight of. Thus, the very last argument for the truth of the cave under the Holy Sepulcher must vanish.

Indeed, as we ascended the hill, which, although  only fifty feet high, is rather steep at the sides, we could look off on either side and see the prominence which such a locality would give an execution. Indeed, the thought came home to our minds so vividly that the very crosses themselves were almost before our eyes. It was a solemn moment ; for to stand where our Lord suffered, and was buried, was to stand upon holy ground.

The American Consul pointed out the place where the ancient Roman gate stood, showing the course the old road took leading up to Damascus, the most frequented route in all that country. The words "All ye that pass by " came strongly to the memory, for we could readily imagine that those who were going into or coming out from the city would naturally raise their eyes to see the criminal on the cross. Thus, when three crosses were one day set there, side by side, and the middle one held the great Teacher of the people, unusual interest must have been displayed. The high city gate, from which the soldiers could get the best view, was crowded, doubtless, with those hardy and hard-hearted men. Throngs stood around the base of the hill, while caravans from the north were arriving at times. Far more than an ordinary execution was this to the people. To the Romans it was the death of one who had defied the Pharisees, and to them it appeared more in the light of a petty execution, which they saw and at once forgot. To the Jews it was the death of one who had exposed their sins. No punishment can equal the hatred of a sinner rebuked. A few sad-faced men stood there trembling, transfixed between fear and grief, while the king, for truly He was a king to die so nobly, expiated the sins of a jeering world.

It needs no very vivid picture of this great sacrifice to prove the utility of right, even if it do conflict with the wishes and convictions of a multitude.

If ever the imagination of man can play without let or hindrance it must burst forth when visiting this spot. Not only will the memory assist, but the surroundings will also force one to pass in review the events of that memorable day. If it is possible for one who understands even the history of that crucifixion, to leave the little hill which looks to-day like the place of a skull without being impressed by his visit, he is beyond the hope of pardon.

Now the top of the hill is smooth, mostly rock

with a little earth, and verdure springing up where
it has a chance. Directly in front is the Cave of
Jeremiah, to reach which it is necessary to descend
the sides of the hill
and walk around. We

find a high, rocky entrance, in which several buildings have been put up, in one of which we discovered the guardian of the cave. He took us within
and showed the inside, which was mainly interesting
from the fact that tradition says Jeremiah dwelt
here and was buried in this place. Near by is the
entrance to the quarries, which are very extensive,
running under the city for a great distance. There
is every reason to believe them exceedingly ancient.
Indeed, there seems little doubt that the stone for
the Temple was quarried here and hewn ready to be
put into place.

But the great interest of the day must lie in the

fact that we had visited Calvary, the very spot, as it seemed to me, on which our Lord was crucified. Indeed, I think all the party felt the dejection of spirit which the thought of that place produced. Even to this day my feelings are still stirred by the vividness with which the whole scene was brought up before my mental vision.

We are thus, by these few things, brought so closely into contact with ancient Jerusalem that, with this for a foundation, the whole city can gradually be built up in the imagination. Taking a few isolated points as a guide we can determine certain outlines, and thus fill in from general reading what we would necessarily desire. The study of ancient sites is one of great interest, and it seems sad to think that we are not permitted to examine the whole ground around the Holy City, since a very little excavation would, without doubt, repay to a wonderful extent. But for many years still the city will remain as it is, unless some great overturning of the present powers of Europe takes place, and leaves some nation free to absorb this country, as justice indeed demands. The rights of the Turk should be respected no longer than he is able to give a fairly decent government to this people. Even were the Syrians allowed to govern themselves, the state of things would be far better.

IV.

An Oriental Hotel.

SOME few years ago we read about travelers who came to Jerusalem and cast about for a lodging ; I believe Mr. Prime was one of these unfortunates. Yet I hardly know whether it is quite correct to say unfortunate, for there were doubtless many experiences which made the search of great worth.   Besides, the experience of living in a native house, in the native style, must have been exceedingly attractive. Then there were other travelers who pitched their tents in true Bedouin fashion outside the Jaffa Gate where we see to-day much that is quaint and oriental.   Of course, the romantic traveler will choose the most inconvenient, and I might say, hence the most attractive way of sojourn.   But for myself there is always a certain romance about a good bed with a tight roof over it. Perhaps this is an instinct born of experience, but it is nevertheless a very comfortable one.

So, while it is prosaic to walk along the street to a hotel just as one might do in Paris or New York, it is, upon the whole, better. I speak advisedly, for, say what one will of this climate, it is never judicious to be exposed to it at night. The Mediterranean Hotel certainly exceeded our ideas of a hotel. Not that it was grander than we had expected, or that it was better, although, perhaps, it was both, but that it was certainly more romantic. Now, of course, romance is attractive only to very young people who have not lost their imagination. But for the sake of the young I must undertake to describe, in very lame fashion I fear, this wonderful structure. Perhaps in so doing I may give some little insight into the way they build Eastern houses.

I always depend a great deal upon first impressions. They give me a certain satisfaction when I look back upon them, which I must say I enjoy. Thus, when the dragoman stopped before a gateway, which was half gate, half door, I felt a little hesitation to enter. In the first place it seemed dark and unwholesome to enter this little narrow alley, at the other end of which I saw only a small stone staircase, which turned when half way up, as though clinging piteously to the wall for fear of falling. Then the gray stone on either side lacked color. In fact, I was a little disgusted, not from any reason, but because—well, because I do like color. I like a picture or something from which a picture can be made. But here it looked like a prison. However, I went in, there was no help for it. We found at the end of the alley a door, square, almost forbidding. Indeed, the view through the doorway was almost repulsive, stone floors, stone walls, and stone ceiling. All gray, hard gray, with that utter lack of color, which only some penitentiary might have.

Thence we passed on a little distance and came to a narrow staircase built into the wall and turning when half way up. At the top we found ourselves in the hotel. Then I was glad I had decided to stay here, for we had discussed the point a little. We emerged into a large room or hall which had at one time been the open court of some fine house. Now it is roofed in with boards brought all the way from the sea. Two ranges of iron balconies led to the rooms, while on the stone floor were placed divans covered with Eastern stuffs, where newspapers, books, and a variety of litter made the whole home-like and cheerful. We were charmed. It seemed like a nest in a wilderness. While there was nothing beautiful, there was everything attractive and comfortable. The previous depression immediately changed into enthusiasm. It seemed as though we had stepped from the commonplace into one of Mrs. Radcliffe's novels. Besides the staircase we had already mounted there were three others : one leading into the dining-room, the others into the drawing-room and to the roof. We, of course, mounted the one going to the top of the house, and in doing so found ourselves on a little platform half way up, which gave us a view quite attractive. Just in the range of vision rose the dome of the

Holy Sepulcher, while the houses which stand around the Pool of Hezekiah came in between. But we, of course, could not wait long to see this scene. The roof claimed our attention. Everywhere it was solid stone—gray, a deep gray in every place, except where the feet of many people had worn it almost white. While on the roof we could look down into the various houses around. The scene which met our gaze I have described before. But now I will take time to speak of our near surroundings. Under our feet the solid stone gave us a sense of safety, while leaning over the iron railing we could see a little how these Eastern houses were constructed. A perfect labyrinth of passages and little courts were spread out before us. In some places a little whitewash, which had turned yellow and brown, gave a bit of color, and my heart warmed at the sight. In front, the Pool of Hezekiah lay deep down in a hole, as it seemed, since it was many feet below us. The water was dark, solemn, and brown. It really looked dirty, and I began to meditate upon the beneficial qualities of such a liquid for drinking. I formed the resolution that I would take wine while I remained in this place. Not that I was sure we did drink the water of this pool, only my fears led me to suspect that by chance I might get some of it. I came so many times to this airy height to see off into the distance, a sight which became much clearer to me as I learned the situation of different buildings in the city, that it seems almost like one of the home spots of the heart. And, indeed, why should it not? In all Jerusalem I doubt if there is a better stand-point. If the hotel were selected because of its elevation, I must applaud the taste of the proprietor. For while I had visited Olivet, I, of course, found it far pleasanter to stand leaning over this railing and muse upon its varied history. Olivet! what a charm lies in that name! I doubt if there are many names which carry so much to the mind and stimulate so greatly the imagination. The fact that I was gazing upon it as it lay there, quiet, peaceful, like some old man with a history, reposing after the busy toil of life, seemed hard to grasp. Its very roughness seemed but the wrinkles and seams of old age, produced not by dissipation, but by hard knocks with the history of the world.

Olivet! How strange as I think of it does

it become ! How unreal to be looking out upon your hillsides, left now to the wandering child of Islam, with your sparse vegetation, your occasional tree, whose very shape shows its antiquity! This is so different from looking at the fanciful creation of some artist, being so commonplace, yes, yet so unreal because my imagination, busy meddler of my brain, will not let me alone. And then the stones around me, how quiet they seem, while I remember that our Lord said even these very stones would have cried out, had not the people recognized him as the King of the Jews. This place seems so small to contain so much. With Olivet there just beside one, as it might seem, and these stone walls lying below, not very grand, not very high, not very numerous, with those hills around it all shutting in the whole scene as a frame does a picture, the mind and the fancy have, perhaps, a freer sweep.

But the idle fancy as fickle as the stray and wandering sunbeam, which now hides itself and again appears, drops down again to the Pool of Hezekiah. Poor Hezekiah ! The history of that time, it seems so hard to comprehend it all ! The armies of the Assyrians spreading themselves over these hills which I see so plainly around ! They could look right down into the city from some points.

Then my mind flits back into the past, trying in one comprehensive grasp to take in all the history of the city from the time that Abraham offered Isaac upon that rock yonder so magnificently clad by the Mosque of Omar, until the present day, when I, a wandering barbarian from the far west, stand high above them all, coming to see with a miserable cockney spirit, or let us hope with reverential feeling. No city ever had so complete a history, so entire a glory, so noble an opportunity, or so ignominious a fate.

But I am tired of letting the mind wander, I have spent enough time up here. The shadows of the evening hour require for a double reason that I go below. It is both tiresome and unhealthy to remain in the night air. So I leave the past, I leave the unrealities behind, and descend for a little while to civilized life, by which I refer, of course, to that miniature England which every native of the British Isle brings with him. And it is a pleasant contrast. It gives the mind a new impulse. I feel a better man for my little communion with antiquity and enjoy the present with keener zest. But if I have to go to my room, perhaps you will accompany me. I ask you because it is so much trouble to get there, that I am sure you will enjoy it. We go down, of course, all the stone steps winding around in a manner which makes me almost forget my way. In fact, if I had not already learned just how to go I should never have dared ask you to go too. Of course, it is easy enough to go down the first flight. One would then think that to reach my room, which is not ten feet off, would be an easy matter. But the fact is I cannot climb a high plastered wall. I can see my door with terrible distinctness, but to reach it I must go down into the main hall, from there down into the stone entrance, out into the alley, then up the little stone staircase, which clings to the wall in such a helpless fashion, through a narrow passage, out into another court, and the door of my room stands before me.

This part of the hotel was once another house, entirely distinct from the main part. It has its court, little fountain, and quiet, secluded air. I could almost imagine I was keeping house there, if it were not so lonesome. The double doors of my room stand half ajar, they have no latch to speak of ; in fact, the only way I can keep them shut is by going inside and putting some kind of a peg into a hole. From the outside it is impossible to do anything more than shut them. Any chance wind will set them open, but it is all right. I thought any lounger from the street could come up this way and take everything I had. But there is no danger, the Arabs for some extraordinary reason do not steal. Within there is a bed with curtains of some kind, a matting on the floor, and a chair. This is comfort. Indeed, I think I am very fortunate to have as much. One little square window looks out upon the Pool of Hezekiah, and it is a great temptation for me, after every one else has gone to bed, to put my head out of this window and look down into the water which is directly underneath. Somehow this water seems more ancient than anything else around here; I presume I was impressed this way by the looks of it. At any rate, I have fine communion with it all by myself, gazing at the black walls on the other side and wondering what they shut out from my view. This is idle curiosity, of course, but I like it so much better than going around among a lot of fictitious places and trying to imagine they are older than I know them to be. After awhile I become tired and go to bed. Fortunately, I sleep well, for if I did not there would be such a crowd of fantasies to dream of that I should be driven distracted.

But I did not ask you, dear reader, to accompany me to find out what I dream. After you have seen my room I will take you back, for you would never get back of yourself, back through all the labyrinth to the hall, where people are beginning to congregate for dinner. It is strange, no matter what may be the romance of a thing, how the mind will inevitably turn with longing toward the dinner hour.

Indeed, perhaps it is just as well to study our surroundings a little. We find a few Englishmen who think it is nice to wear the "fez," or "tarboosh." They think it is becoming, I suppose, and our own Willie has come down in his, a thing he did not dare to do in Cairo, in spite of the fact that it made him look quite handsome, something of which he was not guilty without it. But here in Jerusalem we are so far from London and New York that we need not mind what people think. I cannot say I entirely disapprove, in fact, I should like to wear the tarboosh myself, only a certain pride or feeling that I do not wish to be laughed at prevents me. Then we have the three American girls in our party, of whom I have spoken. They look bright and happy. Indeed, while I have seen many prettier women, I must confess wherever we went these three girls quite took the first rank. Then we have two Hungarians whom we shall know much better before we get through with them ; then a few Germans who are undoubtedly good people, but it takes so long to find out if a German be good, that for a short stay in a place I must admit it does not pay. Then there are others, some of them to be my companions on the long tour, while others who are nice, I trust, make up the whole number, and as the door opens we all troop up the stairs to the dining-room. Behold, here we have a vision. Not that it is a beautiful vision. Mind, I do not say that, but a surprise, something strange. The room is low and arched, and then, singular to

say, covered with frescoes by the hand of a German artist. I need say no more. We feel transported to a German castle. If it were not for the Arab waiters, who are not very expert, it would be difficult to imagine we were not somewhere in the Fatherland.

The whole American party is placed at one end, so we are quite jolly and feel very much at home. We laugh and talk while Willie keeps up an interest by his naïve sayings.

The dinner table is well supplied, and appears in every way European. The majority of travelers are English-speaking, so that we are quite at our ease. The American Consul and his charming wife occupy the head of the table, and make themselves very agreeable to the visitors at the hotel, whether they be American or English. Indeed, the courtesies of these people were exceedingly grateful in a land where kindness is hardly to be expected.

After dinner the guests go their different ways,

and a few remain seated about the hall or in the drawing-room, which is very like the dining-room. The two Hungarians I find are in a conversation with Willie, who thinks he speaks German. As I pass that way he calls to me and introduces me to them, because, as he has found that he can neither understand them nor they him, he does not like to give up the attempt to know them better. Indeed, it always astonishes me to see how little it takes to convince an American that he is a good linguist. Willie did not know more than a dozen words of German, I feel certain, yet he did not hesitate to form an acquaintance with these young men, who were both rich and noble. They had their own especial dragoman, spent their money with a freedom in which only the English and Americans indulge. It was so absurd for this young American boy, for Willie, although very high and very narrow, was only twenty, to walk directly in upon the privacy of these people. If they had been English he would have been well snubbed for his pains. But they were not English-speaking persons, therefore they were courteous, polite, and deferential. While it was quite impossible that they should not have been amused by this boy's impudence, they never showed it in the least. Moreover, I had no very kind feelings toward Willie for the awkward position in which he placed me. As he called me I must, of course, acknowledge the introduction, which was as lame as any I ever went through. Finally, after they had some slight idea what my name was, and while I was wondering from Willie's explanations and their own pronunciation how their names were spelled, I seated myself and tried to be polite. Willie informed me that he had got acquainted and then had found himself unable to proceed with the intimacy he evidently intended to create. I sat aghast. He had pulled me into a pretty situation. I said a few words in German, which they failed to understand. I repeated them, and then they replied. I did not comprehend, and told them so. After they had repeated what they had said, I saw their mean-

ing. Of course the conversation was lame and miserable. I began to wonder if I ever understood German. I re-flected that I had not been in Germany for some months. I took it for granted that they spoke it excellently ; had, in fact, a pure accent, and liber-ally blamed myself. The sit-uation was intolerable. After a few more remarks I left Willie to enjoy the intimacy he had formed, and deter-

mined never to come within speaking distance of these men again. I carried this determination out for several days, and forgot, indeed, for a time, all about the circumstance, in spite of my great mortification.

One day I found it necessary to visit a pharmacy, so went to one outside the walls kept by a German. I hesitated to address him in his native language, but was compelled to do so. He answered me so readily and I understood him so clearly that I felt almost a shock. Could it be that this was German, and that I could both speak and understand it ? I am sure the man must have seen astonishment upon my countenance. I talked with him for some time with perfect ease, and went back to the hotel meditating upon my disastrous encounter with the Hungarians. I saw it all at last. They spoke German with an accent, and, as I afterward learned, with an atrocious one. I, of course, had no accent, and hence our difficulties. Then I quite forgot that they did not speak German at home, but the Magyar language, which is very rough and harsh. I felt much better. My self-pride had been consoled.

I quite understood at last how well it is to be determined in everything. Willie knew nothing of German, yet he plunged in and made two very interesting friends. There were others in the hotel, of course, who helped pass away the time. But it seemed to me that there was nothing so charming as the intricacies of this place, the little passages, the quiet corners, the air of chivalry almost, which was on every side. It was like being entertained in some old castle, a building like those of the Mysteries of Udolpho. With this place for a home and Jerusalem for an occupation I could have remained content all through the summer. While the hotel is generally the lesser part of one's travel, I think it is ofttimes the most interesting. For it is, in fact, that place which temporarily takes the place of home. One's stay in any city must depend greatly upon one's lodgings for its comfort. Thus, I shall have a kindly remembrance of Jerusalem for this one thing, if for no other. Even if some new glaring production from the hand of a European architect is put up near the city, I would still suggest that, even at the expense of a little comfort, it is best to go to the Mediterranean Hotel. Otherwise the charm of the place will be lessened, the beauty of mystery, the quaintness of the Eastern house will be wanting.

V.

Olivet and Bethany.

I CAN think of nothing which brings to the mind a deeper sense of joy than the thought that one is to visit Bethany. One will easily have become accustomed to Jerusalem itself, its dirt, and squalid-looking Arabs, its respectable and intelligent-looking Christians; but the thought that one is to go to Bethany is something new. Somehow the mind reaches far back to the time when Bethany was a pleasant resort for certain weary wanderers, who found there a restful haven from the tumult and trials of the city.

While none need have been sentimental, there

was still a sense of satisfaction, which I feel sure we all possessed, because the little annoyances the party had already undergone were forgotten, and eight of us set out with merry hearts, tempered, of course, by the thought of the sacred spot we were going to visit. As our party came down from the hotel we found that we were to go there on donkeys. In fact, some of us had been asked if we preferred horses or donkeys, and we all agreed that for so short a journey nothing could be more delightful than the smaller animal. Alas! I say it advisedly ; for, while we all set out with the most agreeable feelings, I fear we all came back with a certain bad impression.

But I am anticipating. We had all of us known the Cairene donkey; indeed, after our first experience, I think we had become very much attached to him. So, of course, there was not the least hesitation on our part to ride these donkeys here. Now it is easy enough to ride a donkey, if one knows how. There is only one thing to do, and that is to stay on. It is impossible to guide a donkey, and to this day it remains a perfect mystery to me how I ever went anywhere in particular, or ever came back to my starting point. I lay it to a certain occult influence which the donkey boy has over his charge. We all mounted our animals and started them down the street toward the Jaffa Gate, which was very near by, and found that everything went well. Indeed

we were having a good time.   Why should we not?
Was it not a glorious day, as perfect as was ever
made in celestial work-shops, retouched and gilded
by some master workman, until nothing that even an
artist could desire had been left undone?   My only
regret began to be, that the donkey I rode had not
been made in the same place.   I soon found that
the rest of the party were ahead.   I did not mind this
much, for, as one comes from the Jaffa Gate, there
are many people around, some coming in from the
desert to the south, or traveling, or selling their
wares.   Then there were their booths, with articles
of different kinds, so that the attention was absorbed,
until suddenly I realized that my donkey had a boy
behind him.   I fancy he must have lingered at the
gate for a little chat, for I had not missed him ; indeed, I had not even remembered that every donkey has its boy.   He made himself known by giving
the donkey a tremendous thwack on the flank ; I
am sure I am quite truthful when I say donkey and
rider both went entirely out of the road to what
would have been a gutter in any other place.   I am
a humane man, merciful to beasts, and, while not
exactly a Bergh, I approve of all sorts of happiness
for the brute kind.   Besides, it was very disagreeable to find one's self knocked about in this fashion.
I therefore turned around in some wrath to the boy
and expostulated with him.   He grinned from ear
to ear, and seemed to understand the situation.   I

felt that I had done my duty, when there came
another thwack, and the donkey and rider were
quite knocked over to the other side of the road.
This was too much.   Any man's temper will become
ruffled by being misunderstood, and perhaps one is
more sensitive about being misunderstood in a foreign language.   I turned again
and used all the languages I
knew, I even mixed them up,
so that I afterward reflected
that the most skilled philologist could not have comprehended them.   The boy still
grinned, and did not cease to
beat the donkey.   It was man-
ifestly impossible for me to

talk with him.   I afterward reflected that it is just
as well not to interfere with people.   I arrived at
this conclusion by seeing my party disappear over
the hill, and by observing that my donkey would
not in the least hasten his pace.   I sighed, there
was no help for it.   I have an especial dislike to be
left behind, and I gradually forgot both that I was
a humane man, and that in America there was a
Mr. Bergh.   In short, I became desperate, and the
thwacks which at first seemed to go through me,
hurting me far worse I do believe than they did the
donkey, became, after a while, positive pleasure.   I
even asked the boy for a stick of my own, because

the party had now stopped to wait for me. The boy found a stick, and together we belabored the poor animal until I began to be ashamed. But I still was bound to see Bethany. Had I not had the fondest anticipations, and was I to have a donkey that would not go? But still that donkey would not move off from a walk, and I began to reflect, the most humane thing for Jerusalem would be a society to prevent cruelty to those who have to ride donkeys.

At last I had a brilliant thought. On the lapel of my coat was a pin. I knew it was there, for I always carry one for emergencies. And was not this an emergency? I used it. The donkey seemed to notice it, perhaps as most animals would a fly. The estimation I had of that donkey boy rose every minute. The pin was fast disappearing from useful service, and I was wondering if anything in this world short of a steam engine could make this donkey move out of his leisurely pace. But my party had already gone on, thinking, perhaps, that it was useless to have anything to do with a man who rode so poor a donkey, and I came slowly after. I was growing so angry that I was getting white. The boy and myself exchanged sympathetic glances ; he seemed to grow fond of me, and when a horrid idea came to my mind I looked in his face to see if there was any answering gleam. So far the donkey had not left its leisurely pace, something between a saunter and a complete halt. I remembered, horrible to

relate, but I did remember that within a pocket I
had a knife. I think the idea came slowly at first,
as it was, of course, a prompting of the evil one, and
all sin comes in a sneaking fashion. I think I began to wonder if this donkey actually had feeling.
It was a base curiosity rather than any hope of making him go. Then I thought that five thousand
miles away from Mr. Bergh I was warranted in making what investigations I pleased. Then I fancied
that if I tried the little sharp blade, which I remembered with a distinctness which, I am sure, was born
of the devil, for I find I forget nearly everything
else, it would do no great harm, for the boy would
not and the donkey could not tell.

Altogether it was a grievous sin, but I was sadly
tempted, and I would not risk a single one of my
clerical brethren in the same place and on the same
donkey. In such a case, there would never have
been anything left of the
donkey.

There was only one end
of the matter ; the donkey
did condescend to move
a little more rapidly, and I
caught up with my party,
for they could only go on a
walk, since that gait seems

to have been agreed upon by all the donkeys about
the Holy City. We had now come around the north

of the city wall, passing by the Damascus Gate, and so followed the rough road which led from here down to the Valley of Jehoshaphat. There is not much to see, for on one side is the gray wall of the city and on the other a pile of earth, just high enough to cut off one's view; while in the distance, just across the valley, the Mount of Olives begins to rise. But we followed the wall around the north-eastern corner until we came to St. Stephen's Gate. There we struck into the road which leads down into the valley, which, although not very deep here, has quite steep sides, so that to descend on the back of a donkey might be somewhat hastier than one would desire, especially as so many stones lie in the pathway.

From this spot the view of the valley is interest-ing, because directly ahead the Garden of Gethse-mane lies, and beyond the road to Bethany climbs the hill. Olivet stands above with its three notches, bare and rough, with only a few trees growing in rather stunted fashion along its sides. To the right is the Mohammedan cemetery, which covers the en-tire side of Mount Moriah. Then, as we find our-selves quite at the bottom of the valley, we look about for the brook Kedron, which we have been led to expect here. But it is nowhere to be seen, for the stream exists only when it rains, and there is hardly a channel to show that there should be a brook in this place. To the north of the brook is the Tomb of the Virgin, which the Greeks, who have possession, claim is the oldest church in the world. Just beyond this we come to the Garden of Gethsemane. While it is only by tradition that we place it here, there seems every reason to suppose that this may be the real place where our Lord had the night of agony. It is now about one-third of an acre in size, and is surrounded by a wall of stucco. Eight olive trees stand within its bounds, and are of great age. The ground is laid out in flower-beds ; and the guardian, for a small fee, will give one a bouquet, if it is the season, or a branch of the olive from the tree under which our Lord is said to have passed through His Passion.

While no candid judge of history can accept this as the undoubted location of the Garden of Gethsemane, there is still a certain satisfaction in thinking that, perhaps, here our Lord experienced some of the most solemn moments of His life. The mind goes back with a certain sense of awe, as though it was coming into contact with sacred things, in something of the same manner in which one might approach the uncovered remains of a friend long dead. The monk who tends this garden, so simple and yet so pretty, ought to be a very good man. And, indeed, his gentle looks, his quiet, brown costume, which was tucked up, for he had been working,

6

showed him to be a simple creature, who had, doubtless, been softened by the sight of the dark, frowning walls of the city above, and the gentle, sweet

influence of Olivet
beside him, with all
its touching mem-
ories. The quiet, the
peace, and the free-
dom from care and
excitement, make this
little garden, the
place which our Lord
loved, a sort of
earthly paradise.
Here, too, where na-
ture smiles so lavishly upon human exertion, where
a heaven can be made from scanty materials, there
is a decided satisfaction in living. Would one could
throw off the cares and struggles of life and betake
himself to this peaceful spot, and spend his life in
following the different courses which Jesus took
about this city ; he might then bring himself to an
enviable state of peace and joy. But bidding the
good and kind old monk adieu, we went without to
find our donkeys, which were left with their attendants, and the sight of them brought us back again
to the miseries of earth.

We left Gethsemane behind with regret, for it is
one of the peaceful things about Jerusalem, and

began to climb the Mount by means of a steep and somewhat winding road, which was washed and seamed by the rains of early winter. But our donkeys scrambled on with commendable courage and they soon brought us to the mosque, situated in a small village which occupies the central part of the Mount. Within a large courtyard we leave our donkeys and ascend a minaret, standing brownish-yellow in the sunlight, which, coming now from the west, gives deep shadows, such as an artist loves, and brings out into prominence the picturesque effect of the tower. It is not much of a climb, but it is a difficult thing to keep one's position on a windy day, and this day the breeze had full sweep over the hills of Judea, and was stopped by no obstruction as it came from the sea. The first sight from the tower is one which it is impossible to forget. Of all the maps I have ever seen, none can equal the one nature has made here. The Holy City stands out in perfect clearness, apparently just by one's feet, every part in plain view. I begin to realize why Jerusalem is called the Beautiful, for a more perfect picture could not be made. This is a position of the greatest advantage for getting a full and complete idea of its topography. The plain or uneven tableland which comes down from the north seems

gradually to lower itself until the uppermost wall
of the city begins. Then a spur shoots suddenly
out, forming the Mount Zion, which makes a kind
of semicircle, in the hollow of which lies the city
itself, with the Temple Area as a sort of central
point. The Mosque of Omar forms the pivot, and
the wall of the enclosure breaks off abruptly,
so that all the city seems to start from this point,
and is thus more easily comprehended in its details.
If this picture satisfies, what must have been the
effect when Solomon's great Temple stood in the
same conspicuous place? There is now a grandeur,
an imposing and regal air to the whole scene, which
I have in vain sought for from other standpoints.
Not even from the other road, the way we shall
return to Jerusalem, was the city so grand. Here
every house seems clearly visible, the eye easily
singling out the Tower of David, quite on the western side of the city. St. Stephen's Gate and the
eastern wall are now but a huge pedestal on which
the city seems reared, while the Valley of Jehoshaphat seems a moat cut out to give the city importance. At this distance the soft effect of the atmosphere is dimming the rough hardness of the colors,
until there is a witchery about the grayness and
the brown, which we had not before discovered.
Then, too, the western hills, which show a little of
their tops in the distance, have the tinge of warm
sunlight, which turns their bluish gray almost to

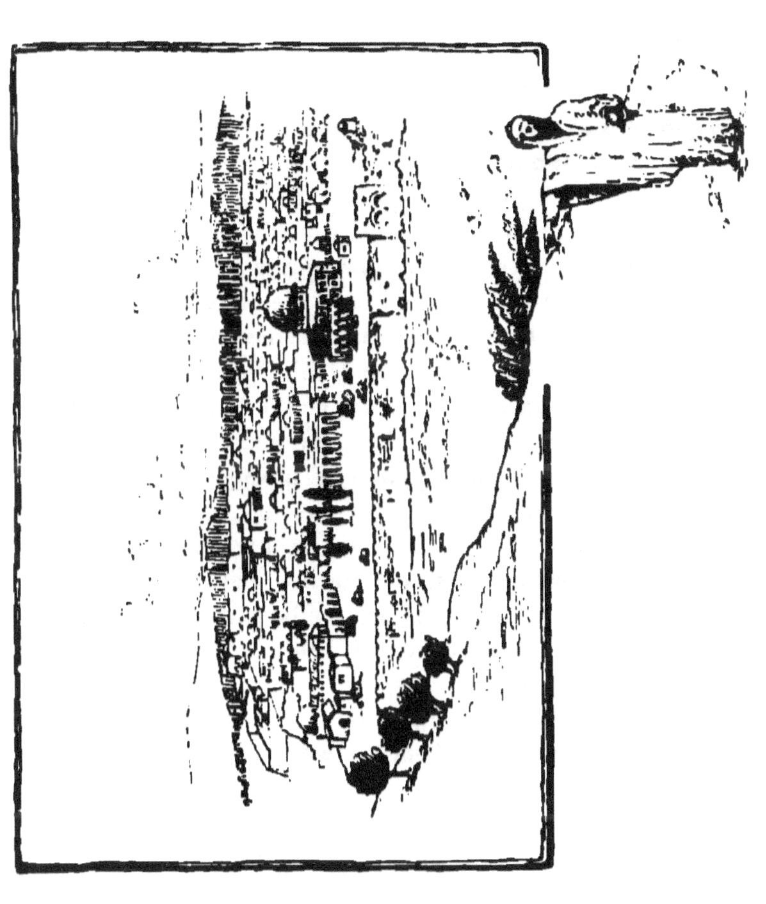

some delicious green. Toward the north, enchanted land of Damascus, there is a hardness of color which only brings out the softness of the rest of the scene ; while directly under us are gardens, not seen until now, and a few, very few, busy people, which give life to the picture.

It is easy to think of the hostile armies, which have in time past occupied this spot and looked down upon this city. Never could there have been a more advantageous place for such a scene, because never could a great city have been so commanded, and yet, from its position, so impregnable in those times. But, as we are struggling to maintain our hold on the narrow balcony around the top of the tower, we see the boys and the Arabs bickering in the courtyard below. It is always amusing to see Arabs dispute. They make so much noise and mean so little by it. However, we are not here to watch them, so we go around to the other side and take the view to the east, down the hills of Judea, and the wadies to the Dead Sea, which can, I believe, be discerned from this point ; Moab and Gilead, the hill of Evil Counsel, and the Valley of Rephaim. We turn away with regret, but as we were to see all these places more closely we could not linger longer. So we descend, mount our donkeys and come to the curious church built by a French princess on the spot where our Lord taught the disciples to pray. In the court are thirty-three tiles, each with the Lord's Prayer in a different language inscribed thereon. Here she built her future tomb, and I confess I had a pleasant sympathy with her in desiring to spend the future near the Holy City.

But we must hasten on to Bethany, which lies just to the other side, on the eastern slope of the Mount of Olives. The road is miserable, and the way at times steep and difficult, seeming so because we were not well accustomed to Palestinian roads. But our donkeys take us safely, since, if they are not fast, they are certain. Almost before we knew it we entered the town, and found ourselves among a lot of the most miserable and squalid houses I have ever seen. And, although I have since become very accustomed to the filth of the East,  this place lingers in my memory as the very worst I ever saw. The streets are so uneven and miserable, and withal so narrow, the houses so dilapidated and cheerless, and the inhabitants so utterly forsaken and sickly in appearance, that it seems as though the choicest spots of our Lord's ministry have become, by some fatality or curse, the vilest dens on earth. The shock to one's feelings is so great, that for a time it seems a fearful thing to visit Bethany.

There is nothing in the place to indicate that there
was ever an atom of decency there. A tower is
shown, which is called the castle of Lazarus, and
also a vault which is said to be his tomb. We went
down into it by the help of a candle, pulling our
clothes up around us for fear of contamination.
Within there was nothing of interest, just the bare
stone of what was once doubtless an Arab tomb.
Dogs made life unendurable, and the sullen countenances of the natives gave one a feeling of dread.
All is desolation, and to think of our Lord and the
gentle Mary, or the industrious Martha, in a place
of such abandoned laziness, seems well nigh a pro-
fanation. It was with a feeling of delight that we
turned our donkeys' heads toward Jerusalem. It
was much better to imagine than to see the reality
of this place. So we found ourselves going over
the stony road, which became more and more so as
we proceeded around the southern end of the mountain, until we approached that point where our
Lord saw the city and wept over it. After we could
forget Bethany and reflect upon that memorable
journey, we found great pleasure in looking at the
landscape, for there is no doubt about the identity
of this spot. The crowd of people, the shouts and
the palm branches, were all clearly visible, the
meek, sinless man, riding upon an ass, the procession as it neared the city, all is vivid as you ride
over these rough roads. While the country is not

now beautiful, and while the brown earth is rarely covered with verdure, the shape of the hills must remain the same. When our Lord passed through this familiar scene, beautiful with every art of a royal ruler, flourishing with every flower and shrub which this climate brings forth, the thought of destruction came to Him like a flash of light as He saw that vision which burst upon His view ; a vision even now to one who has not seen it before, the only point of view from which the Temple looms up in majesty.

It is necessary to pause to comprehend how our Lord felt at this sight. For directly in front is

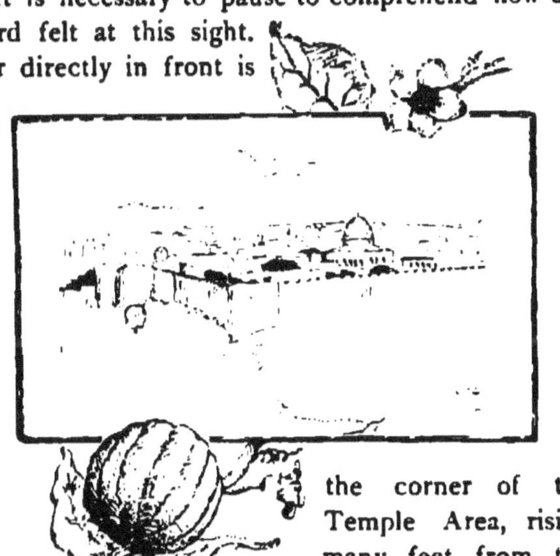

the corner of the Temple Area, rising many feet from the valley beneath, which here cuts down so deep into the earth as to make this corner remarkably high. Then in that time, when the débris of so many sieges had not filled up the depth, it was even more imposing. Above this rose the Temple in its splendor, ornamented and set off by every kind of architectural skill. To the left on Mount Zion was the palace of Herod, even more imposing than the Temple, because so much higher, while back of it all rose the buildings of the city, no mean sight, if we may believe half of what was written. To-day we see but part of this scene ; the Mosque of Omar, which, although beautiful in itself, is nothing to what the Temple was ; the barren valley, the waste hillsides, the seared appearance of the land, as if the fire brand had passed over it and left it to desolation ; the sadness of this destruction, the meek appearance of the city sitting in sackcloth and ashes, vile in her degradation, cursed by her sin, hopeless for regeneration. All this comes over one and more, more than words can tell, more than imagination can fancy.

So we go down the hillside, expecting every moment that the small feet of the donkey will precipitate us to the stones. But fortunately it is all right, and we find ourselves at last after much anxiety in the valley below. Here we pass the Tomb of Absalom, and see nothing but the tombs of buried Mussulmans around us with their queer head-stones. To mount the opposite side and enter the Dung Gate is a difficult task both for the

donkey and the rider. But my mercy is gone, a
deep sense of hatred has taken possession of me,
though on all subjects except donkeys I adjudge
myself as good a Christian as ever. A ride through
the bazaars is in a sense comforting, for I am near-
ing the hotel, and there I have the cheerful prospect of bidding farewell to this donkey forever.

VI.

Picturesque Views.

THERE is much to see in Jerusalem, and yet little
which is really worth description. I felt that my
visit was of most benefit to me by showing me the
topography of the city, and setting right the distorted ideas which I had gained. Thus I did not
spend so much time in seeking for the sights, as I
did in wandering around by myself, and absorbing
the atmosphere of the place. It is hardly possible to
get lost anywhere in the vicinity, and the distances
are not so great that one cannot easily walk. Thus
I had an opportunity which I had not had before in
Eastern cities. I esteem myself extremely fortunate
that I could wander about Jerusalem, for I know
no place so well adapted to a meditative excursion.

It may seem strange that an abundance of good

maps and careful descriptions, together with a plas-
ter model of the city, should not give one a very
good idea of the place. But I remember that I had
occasion once to give quite an extended account of
the Valley of Jehoshaphat in connection with the
healing of the blind man, who was sent to the
waters of Siloam. The pool, of course, claimed its
share of my attention, and while I was not exactly
wrong, and had said nothing which could be criti-
cised, I saw at once that my ideas were false. It was
then with considerable curiosity that I set out one
morning with my donkey—it was not the same I had
ridden to Bethany, needless to say—and together we
took our reflective way down the street from the
Mediterranean Hotel. I say reflective in connection with the donkey, because that is, beyond a
doubt, the word which best describes its appearance.
It is enough to set one thinking simply to watch
the animal for a short time. It may be just possible, as these were meditative animals, that is why
they could not be brought to a trot or gallop, as
in Cairo, where donkeys are more frivolous. This
animal was large and strong. Indeed I felt none
of those soft sensations of pity which I had previously experienced. I rode him as I would a war
horse, only less rapidly, of course, and pounded
him to my heart's content. The boy could not
disturb my equanimity by his occasional thwacks,
because of the size and general importance of his

charge.   Thus I proceeded with all dignity through that street just by the hotel (I do not remember the name, and indeed I see no use in doing so), where the Arabs sat in great state, smoking their tchibouks, and eyeing me with a cool contempt which was hard to bear.   But then I was an Englishman to them, of course an American in reality, and I enjoyed all the prestige of my Anglo-Saxon countenance.   The terror of the English name is more potent far than anything else in this benighted land.

So turning at the corner of the street I find myself very soon opposite the Church of the Holy Sepulcher.   It is impossible not to stop just a moment and look at the interior.   The graceful architecture of the tomb with its dome, and the vast space of the larger dome which covers it, gives one a feeling of awe.   If one realizes that only a few years ago the strife between Christians was so great in this place that two hundred were killed, the respect for the warring sects is decidedly diminished.   But, perhaps, the handsomest part of the whole building is the nave proper, which is devoted to the Greek worship.   The style of decoration is more chaste and regular, and exhibits more attention than the Sepulcher itself, which, being in the hands of several opposing factions, thus escapes the attention it should naturally have.

In a moment I have returned to my donkey and resumed my tour of investigation.   The Via Dolorosa is just at hand, and down this solemn road I steer my donkey's head, or the boy does it for me. It is not well authenticated, for, before the fourteenth century, it was entirely unknown. Then, too, as the Holy Sepulcher is now generally considered to be a place assigned by tradition, having no real basis in fact, we may ride along this street without any great feeling upon the subject. If, indeed, our Lord had passed this way, it would have been to every Christian a most solemn thing to trace His footsteps. But now we honor only the invention of men. While much superstition has gathered about this place, there has also been much artistic thought spent here, for many pictures have taken this street as a ground-work in which to represent the greatest suffering the world has ever seen. Thus we bow to Art if we cannot bow to Truth.

The narrow street, which here and there has some archway thrown across, whose high walls stand gloomy beside one, can give much food for reflection. The touching devotion of those who believe, if nothing else, should fill the soul with religious feeling. For it seems to me that, next to religion itself, comes the faith in another, a faith which moves one to hardship and trial, and hence to a discipline of spirit, which is the foundation of all true loveliness. How many have gazed on the blackened stone where Lazarus sat! How many have looked up to the window where Dives was wont to look forth, and how many have stooped to kiss the spot where our Lord fell under the burden of the cross!

So we come at last to St. Stephen's Gate, which has been called by this name since the middle of the

fifteenth century, because it was stated by tradition, founded upon a dream of a priest in the fourth century, that it was without this gate St. Stephen suffered. The Damascus Gate toward the north had been previously known by this name. Thus we can get some insight into the value of tradition in placing the sites of our Lord's time.

Without the gate the road divides into four or five branches, the one we shall take turning sharply to the right along under the city wall and through the Mohammedan cemetery. The tombs lie in every direction, having the queer head pieces which are supposed to be turbans, but which are usually so badly executed as to excite wonder. The wall of the Temple stands so gray and rugged, and the graves of deceased Mussulmans are so gloomy that one must be sadly reflective, even if the slow, contemplative movements of the donkey did not impel one to this cast of thought.

The Valley of Jehoshaphat below grows gradually deeper, and as we reach the Golden Gate we turn down the steep path leading into it. The way is stony, but the donkey is sure, and so very slow that no thought of danger can enter the mind. At last, for it is no little trip on a donkey, we find ourselves before the Tomb of Absalom, so well known in pictures of the Holy Land. Recent examination has proved beyond a doubt that it is entirely Greek in its architecture, and was not known until the twelfth century by this name. However, the pile of stones which pious people have thrown against it, as some feeble expression of disapproval for disobedience in a son, should teach every man who has a father a powerful lesson. Very near is the so-called Tomb of St. James. Recent discoveries show it to belong to the family of Beni Hezir. Apparently it dates from the first century before Christ.

Here the valley still descends, having the village of Siloam on the left, while on the right is the Fountain of the Virgin. This is reached by going

7

down thirty steps, and has been regarded as a possible site of the Pool of Bethesda. Recent exploration has shown that it is connected by an  underground channel with the Pool of Siloam. The exploration of this tunnel was extremely difficult, and the glory of it really belongs to an Arab boy, who went through and reported that he had seen writing within. Acting upon this information, three men interested in the work of exploration plunged into the tunnel armed with everything necessary to make a copy, and returned with the most interesting Hebrew inscription ever found in Palestine. It is now admitted to be as old as the time of Solomon, and explains the meeting of the two parties, who, in digging the tunnel from opposite ends, met midway.

" Behold the excavation. Now this is the history of the tunnel. While the excavators were still lifting up the pick toward each other, and while there were yet three cubits to be broken through, the voice of one called to his neighbor, for there was an excess in the rock on the right. They rose up. They struck on the west of the excavation. They struck each to meet the other, pick to pick. And there flowed the waters from their outlet to the pool for a thousand two hundred cubits, and .... of a cubit was the height of the rock over the heads of the excavators."

This makes a very interesting study, even if one do not take the pains to enter the tunnel for himself. By mere chance we are hrought back into the centuries, touching, as it almost seems, the very hem of Solomon's robe. The Pool of Siloam lies five hundred yards below, and we find upon looking

that it is a reservoir fifty-three feet long and eighteen feet wide. The waters flow intermittently, which is explained by the tunnel which has so recently been explored. Here the blind man came and washed. The poor creature, feeling his way along, coming with that simple faith, goes down into the pool without  hesitation, secure of recovering his sight. This is a touching picture, for there exists no doubt of this locality. Down these steps he must have come nearly two thousand years ago, and I stand on the same spot where his feet and so many other feet have trod.

Yet to-day the water is quite like other water. The edges of the pool are in a ruinous condition. Age, extreme age, is all around. The city seems very high above, almost hidden from this spot. So

I remount my donkey, with increased reflection I urge him up the steep side of Zion, scarcely pitying him as I should another animal, and slowly,

yet rapidly enough for me in my present state of mind, I find myself going along under the walls. To the left on the outer edge of the Mount is the house of Caiaphas and David's Tomb. Within the house of Caiaphas we may find a pleasant courtyard. The custodian is a marvel in himself. Large, rotund in the truest sense of the word, he just manages to show people around. It is a pleasant house, but then Caiaphas never saw it. I simply gaze at it as a piece of Eastern architecture. While the old man is showing the rest of the visitors around I seize the opportunity of making a little sketch of him. Poor, unconscious old man, you little knew how far your figure would travel !

In the mass of buildings around David's Tomb is the chamber where the Last Supper was held, according to tradition. I will say nothing more about it, than that it is profitable to those that have the charge, and I visited it through the worship of a fetich, one to which Americans bow down, the seeing of sights.

It is pleasant to linger along under this wall, for, fortunately for me, the sun has been unusually good-natured during my stay in the Holy City. Thus I enjoy my little saunter along the wall, with the great Tower of David rising before me. I look complacently down into the Valley of Hinnom, I see the travelers coming up the road from Bethlehem ; the people around the Jaffa Gate ; and at last I must myself go in, for I have done enough for one afternoon.

VII.

Bethlehem.

On Saturday we were to go to Bethlehem. The ride was to be taken on horseback, both because this was the easiest mode of reaching the place, and because we were then to try our horses, to learn if they would be agreeable for the long journey through the country. This is a matter of so much importance that I regret to say the principal interest in taking this excursion lay in that fact. We had now been in the Holy City long enough to become *blasé* in a measure, and could hear of a stroll on Mount Zion or a little excursion to Olivet without being shocked, as most people are at first, because of the sacred associations.

But perhaps the most important part of my journey now came up before me in rather startling colors.

Hitherto I had taken whatsoever came to me with good nature, and saw only kindly intentions and a good disposition in the agent and dragoman belonging to Mr. Cook's establishment. With the journey to Bethlehem my eyes began gradually to be opened. But to begin properly ; we were highly delighted by the information given us by the agent, who was, as I have said, an American, a fact I resented bitterly, that we were exceptionally lucky, for we were to have the horses the Duke of Sutherland's party had just relinquished. What could be more delightful, especially to our English friends, than to ride the same horses these distinguished persons had ridden! Then, of course, after the thought of so near a contact with the nobility, came the satisfaction of knowing that the duke would have none but the best animals.

So, with these ideas in mind, I walked around the hotel, serene, happy and contented ; because I am very fond of a good horse, if I have to ride him, one which will go fast, freely, and well. I prepared myself for the ride, and waited for the rest of the party to gather together. At last, it was after the midday meal, we all trooped down the stairs out into the alley, and so into the street, which was so narrow as to be another alley. In front of the hotel opened the little square on which the Bishop's Palace, as it is called, the English Church, and the Tower of David stand. The horses were tied around this inclosure, and I stopped astonished as I gained the first view of them. Then I walked all around, looked them all over in a sort of stupor. These the horses the Duke of Sutherland had ridden! Miserable man, to have no better judgment than this! I examined the animals more closely. At last I found one which did not seem quite so much gone to pieces as the others, and calmly said I would take him. The dragoman remarked that that did not belong to our party, in fact was owned by an Arab chief. I looked around on the rest, but a more jaded, tired, miserable lot of horses I had never seen. It seemed an actual cruelty to mount them. Then I saw sores, wounds, cuts, everything in fact which renders a horse ill-looking. I was so disappointed that I did not find an opportunity to be angry. I shrank from riding beasts so miserable. The only word which accurately describes their condition is, shabby. It was quite true. They were actually coming to pieces. The hair was gone in places, the skin more often, and they were bound up in a way which reminded one of a hospital. I was a little ahead of my party and thus had a certain priority of choice. I selected the best-looking one of the lot and was coolly informed that it was already taken. Then I searched for another. My choice was by this time restricted to two or three mere skeletons. I took the pleasantest-looking animal, and setting my teeth together, mounted to its back, where I used all my self-control to keep from pitying the animal too much. The party started, the most forlorn, the most dejected I have ever seen. Fortunately most of the company had ridden but little before, and the quiet character of the horses rather suited them.

So we rode out of the Jaffa Gate, while the stiff limbs of our animals, and they were all lame at first, gradually became more limber, and pursued our way down the hill leading from the Jaffa Gate into the Valley of Gihon. This is perhaps the only road about Jerusalem which does not need some urgent repair. It descends gradually until it crosses the valley at the upper end of the Lower Pool of Gihon, and then ascends the hill, leaving on the left the traditional tree on which Judas hanged himself, and the country house of Caiaphas the High Priest. The plain into which the road now extends has been called the Valley of Rephaim. This is the spot where David defeated the Philistines. I found when I reached this place that my horse had recovered the use of his limbs and could canter. So the younger members of the party hurried forward with little regard either for the comfort of our horses or that of the ladies, who were following, and who deemed it necessary to keep up with us. The road is for the most part level, with occasional rises, and the country seemed an improvement upon that which we had seen. The early spring vegetation was just showing its greenish tinge, while over all the fields there lay innumerable stones, which must greatly annoy the tiller of the soil. Just before we reached Bethlehem we came to the Tomb of R a c h e l, which stands amid a certain desolation. The t h o u g h t that there is l i t t l e doubt about its being the true site makes one still more sad than the dilapidated appearance of the tomb i t s e l f. The

sweet character of this daughter of Laban, and the touching love-story of her life must appeal to all hearts, when one comes in sight of this monument, which, though not grand in itself, still bears witness to the reverence of both Moslems and Christians.

The approach to Bethlehem does not, I fancy, equal that which the imagination has pictured. While it lies in the inner curve of a semicircle, the style of building, the general shabbiness, to one as yet unaccustomed to the general decay of the East, seems in a way mournful. It is difficult to imagine that night, long years ago, when the people were flocking to this place to be enrolled in their proper tribe ; when the rich men from the far East were coming with their gifts ; when the bright star was shining upon the group of people ; when the shepherds were sitting out under the clear night looking,

doubtless, at this wonderful star.   It is difficult to
see how so many people could sustain life from so
sterile a soil, how Bethlehem could be a city at all.

But we ride into
the town almost
without thought,
for in the first
place all is so
commonplace,
so tame, and so
very real.   The
narrow, filthy
street, whose
urchins look up
in a kind of half
scorn, and with
very little inter-
est ; the low
houses, appar-
ently half built,
all give one an
idea that it is a very dilapidated place after all.

Quite at the other end of a rather long street is
situated the Church of the Nativity.   A large open
place in front of it adds to the fortress-like effect
of the vast pile of buildings which bears this name.
One would hardly fancy that within there were
aisles and a nave.   The horses stop at a small door,
so small and narrow as to be utterly insignificant,

when compared to the great mass of buildings to
which it is the entrance. But we are informed
that this ignoble entrance used to be necessary
to prevent the attacks of the Arabs. Passing
within we find ourselves in a large, and once splendid church. It is said to be the old-
est monument of Christian architecture i n
t h e world,
and is the
sole remain-
i n g p o r-
tion of the
grand basil-
ica w h i c h
t h e E m-
press Hel-
ena erected

here in 327 A. D. It is imposing, even
in its decay. The five rows of columns
are still grand, and the mosaics show
remnants of great beauty. The roof
is formed of cedar beams brought from
Lebanon. But it is dingy, faded, and old. While
vast, imposing, and suggestive of past glory, it is a
fitting monument of that kind of Christianity which,
let us hope, is relegated to the past. No instance
of an enormous, expensive building could show so
clearly the folly of erecting to God that which has

no earthly use.   Unless men can see in the ages to
come that Christianity is for man, and not for God,
I fancy that religion will perish from off the earth.
To-day one stands in this edifice, which in point
of size is justly comparable with any churches in the
world, and wonders what rash folly ever possessed
the good Empress to waste so much money.   It is
so dreary, so cold, so deserted, so utterly the shell

of Christianity, that Christianity seems a very farce
right here where it began.   Indeed it is a powerful
lesson to men, to understand that Christ came not
upon earth for any reason of sentiment, but to give
the world a real and practical good.   If the very
spot of His birth has become the center of a wrang-
ling mass of Christians, so greedy, so bigoted, so
rapacious, that heathen power must intervene to
keep them apart, how far have they strayed from
that simple Disciple of Peace, Who would not, even

to save Himself from death, evoke the passions of the people.

But if the mind is filled with thoughts of the folly of Christians while walking up and down the stretches of this dreary waste of building, the heart is certainly moved to gentleness to think of that birth which took place some centuries ago under these very stones. The thought, that this is indeed the spot where the greatest civilization of the world saw its birth, should be enough to touch the skeptic heart, while the Christian should of course have far higher and nobler emotions. Still I hesitate to penetrate into that cave, sacred for so many centuries, for there I am aware I shall meet the gaudy, the tawdry, the idolatrous, all that makes a truly artistic heart rebel. This old church stripped of its glory is far better, for here at least we have the grandeur of proportion, God's own skill, without those flimsy adornments which the narrow mind of man fancies beautiful.

But then of course one must go. That is always the curse of traveling. One never has the self-respect or strength of character to refuse to visit places which his common sense forbids. So as there are two spiral stair-cases which lead down to the cave, which is just twenty feet below the pavement, we descend one of them and find ourselves in a vault thirty-three feet long by eleven wide, lined all around with Italian marble, and decorated by lamps, figures

of saints, embroidery and other trivialities. It is
quite as I expected, only perhaps a little exaggerated.

I did not ex-
pect to see
Italian marble
here of all
places in the
world, and the
designs, too,
are in the worst
possible taste.
Instead of see-
ing the cave
as it should
be, bare, with
the rough rock, which would then have had some
attraction, we are treated to the inventions of half-
educated monks. A silver star shows the place
where our Lord was born. But it is no use to try
and imagine that event. The care taken to cover
up everything which is natural, is only equaled by
certain branches of the Christian Church to hide
nearly every bit of true Christianity. There is no
interest in the altar, plain and bare, nor in the lamps
which the Latins, Armenians and the Greeks have
hung around.

At one side is the Chapel of the Manger, another
piece of tawdriness ; then the Altar of the Magi ;
the Chapel of Saint Joseph ; the Altar of the Inno-

cents, and the so-called Tomb of Eusebius. The truthfulness of the site can hardly be questioned, since it has not only the authority of very early tradition, but was accepted by Justin Martyr one hundred years after the events happened. Then it has the probability of circumstance, since it is extremely likely that the caves around here were used for stables when the inn itself was full.

Perhaps one of the most touching things connected with this place is the devotion of Saint Jerome. With that holy zeal and devoted love, which was so pre-eminently the characteristic of the Early Church, he came to this spot and made for himself a home in a cave in this very rock in which our Lord was born. For more than thirty years he toiled, prayed, dreamed and studied. Here he gathered around him the communities of monks, which were scattered so greatly through the country in after times, and left as his great work the Vulgate of the Latin Church, the first translation into Latin of the Hebrew Scriptures. Perhaps no man stood up so strongly for the Scriptural interpretation of the Word of God. And we have to thank him for keeping the Church in the right path, instead of straying off into other ways through the influence of heathen philosophy.

After we had gazed long enough at the various altars and places of commemoration, we passed into the Franciscan Monastery, where we saw the table set out for both visitors and the regular inmates of the place. It looked homelike. The monk who went with us seemed kind, and I felt that to spend a time within these walls would at least be interesting if not romantic. After lingering a while, without any desire to visit the Milk Grotto or the Shepherd's Field, we returned to the open place where our horses had been standing with some Arabs to hold them. The sun was shining softly, warm enough for us to dispense with our outer coats, and as we gathered around our animals we felt a certain sense of happiness, a kind of relief, I fancy, to be quite out of this place of bigotry and superstition. The fact that our Lord was born there did not appeal to us so strongly as it ought. The realities of everyday life are too great, too appealing for us to overlook them. Especially was this the case when I discovered that through the girths of my saddle the blood was oozing. I immediately ordered them to be removed, and lo ! a most horrid sore appeared which the groom, whoever he was, had so covered up when we started that I could see nothing of it. I was so filled with horror that I upbraided the dragoman in such a manner that he promised me another horse for the long journey. Then I fell into a chat with one of my companions about riding, and he disclosed the fact that his horse was something atrocious to ride. I offered to exchange with him and he accepted. Indeed I had noticed his antics as we were coming out, and I felt sorrow as well as amusement to think he had not learned in his youth the way to ride a horse. However, when I had once mounted the beast, which was, I am happy to say, comparatively whole, I found that even an expert rider must use a great deal of tact to get along comfortably. But as I had no sympathy for a horse whose profession was being ridden, and which did not fulfill its engagements better than this, I put him through his paces, and with the other young men of the party I had a merry time on our way back to the city. We were obliged to pass through the long street, the only one I believe which the town possesses, and then as we came into the open country we stopped a moment to see the fountain of which David longed to drink when the Philistines occupied Bethlehem. Three mighty men, hearing his wish, broke through the Philistine hosts and brought him the desired draught. But David, noble-souled man that he was, refused to drink that which had imperiled the lives of his brave followers, and poured it out before the Lord.

The old gentleman, whose pretty daughter was one of our party to Bethlehem, and with whom I had been in Cairo, wishing to visit the place went there in a wagon. And while the journey was all right for part of the way, the latter half proved troublesome because of the stones in the road. How he with his infirmities ever stood it I cannot understand. His daughter declared she saw him thrown two feet into the air at one moment, and sitting quite still at another. But as she was a bright, lively girl, she may have exaggerated. But as we passed through the fields, on every hand the view became better as we neared the city. The road was freer from stones, and the young men dashed on, until coming to the English Consulate, which stands opposite Mount Zion, on the other side of the valley, we all paused to rest before we made the final gallop into the city. The rest of the party followed us. Jerusalem seemed like a home, and the part of the city lying in our direction presented a better aspect than the other side, which is entirely given over to the Moslems.

VIII

The English in Jerusalem.

JERUSALEM is to-day so much the city of foreigners that the Moslem element seems hardly to have a
hold upon the place.   Within the last few years great
improvements have been made, handsome buildings
have been erected, the streets have no longer that air
of complete decay which always marks Mohammedan sway. Especially do the newer buildings, those
of the Russians, Germans and English, give the city
a new aspect.   Without the walls are already large
and spacious dwellings used by the English people
connected with the missions there.   Indeed the different consulates, and the air of prosperity that this

suburb has already attained, threaten to overshadow the city itself.

I fancy the dominant influence which England and Russia have had at the Porte has greatly encouraged this progress. Formerly it was not only unsafe to build, but it was difficult to hold property. Now it seems tacitly conceded by the Turkish Government that foreigners may possess the city of Jerusalem. Especially does an American find advancement in the English ranks. Within the walls is a beautiful English Church built in the Gothic style, comfortably large, and supplied with all the appliances needful for its purpose. At first sight one almost wonders what necessity there is for a building so large and so fine. But the day I preached there the church was filled to its utmost extent, entirely with people who dwelt in the place, having of course a few travelers interspersed. I was astonished, because I could hardly understand where so many English-speaking people came from. There was no especial reason why they should be present in such numbers, and I concluded that it was a usual occurrence.

As this was my first experience in an English pulpit, I was somewhat annoyed by the strange, old-fashioned way in which it was arranged. I had never been in it, so when the time came to preach I was shown a door which led into darkness. I plunged in, discovered a flight of steps, and emerging into the desk found myself raised so far above the congregation, that it must have been very uncomfortable for them to listen to me. As for myself, I simply leaned over the cushion and took a bird's-eye view of them.

The clergyman, who is at the head of the church, is at the same time master of the schools, which have been established here by the London Society for the Conversion of the Jews. His duties, I fancy, consist only in superintending. He receives a thousand pounds for his services, and has a large and very comfortable house without the walls in the Frank quarter. It was my good fortune to be invited to his house and to meet his family. With true English conservativeness they had brought England with them. Although the house outside showed the influence of native taste in architecture, and the hall was perhaps a little cold because so solidly built of stone, yet the drawing-room was as truly homelike as any we would find in England. The ladies were English in the sense that they were cordial and kind, and the evening I spent with this family was a truly delightful oasis in a journey, but little relieved by seeing the home life of friends. While, of course, there is a great deal of isolation, still there is considerable society in a quiet way, and the life of a missionary in Jerusalem cannot be hard.

I visited the native church, which is near by, at the same time, going with the American Consul, at that time Dr. Merrill, who was everything that politeness and courtesy could be, and saw that only a few of the natives were in attendance. The church is fine, indeed fine enough for our own land. The building, being built entirely of stone, because wood is so dear, presented so solid and respectable an appearance that I could not but reflect that there were many places both in England and America, where there are far larger congregations which require such an edifice more than it is needed here. I think the missionary was a native. At any rate, the preacher I heard was an Arab, and those who could understand said the sermon was a good one.

There is also a large orphanage and school for Arab children, which I visited. It stands on Mount Zion, on that end which the present city does not cover. The head master, who was a clergyman, seemed sickly and tired. I fancy that the task of getting English ideas into Arab heads is more difficult than we imagine. We sat for a while in the parlor waiting his coming, for I visited this school with the English gentleman, whom I shall henceforth call the Philologist, since he was an author well known for his books on this subject. While we were waiting he said to me, as he saw me tapping my fingers on the arm of the chair I was occupying:

"Where is your knife?"

"In my pocket," I replied.

"But don't mind me," he said.

"Mind you?" I asked in some surprise.

"Yes, I do not care, you may whittle if you wish."

"Thank you," I said a little sarcastically, I fancy, for I could not quite understand his innuendoes.

"Do not all Americans whittle?" he asked mischievously.

"I never have," I replied smiling.

"I thought they were never happy unless they were." The wife of the master came in, I was introduced, and we went to visit the school-rooms. Everything was exactly as it would be in an English school, the same neatness, the same regularity, and the same uninteresting appearance, only the faces of the scholars were dark and keen.

This is the result of missions. It has practically resolved itself into education. It is evident to careful people that the only way to Christianize is to bring up the ignorance of heathendom to our own level of wisdom, and then we may have some small chance of bringing them over to our belief. Let a careful man calculate the mass of ignorance in one of these lands, and then calculate the number of pupils in a country, and he will have some little idea how much work our missions are at present doing for the hea-

then. Certainly there was nothing encouraging in
this school, when one reflected that it was English
money, English push and energy, and simply com-
placence on the part of the natives as an offset. I
cannot divest myself of the idea that the miserable
Londoners of the East End would have turned this
education to a far greater advantage.

Then we went to the German institution for
deaconesses. This was a sort of missionary journey of ours, tramping around to see what we could
of missionary work. At this place, a large building
which partook of the German solidity and ugliness,
and Arab commonplace, we were received by a
bucket of water coming toward us from the rear of
the hall. We had appeared at a wrong moment,
for the cleaning, which makes this place delightful
inside, was just commenced. We waded through
the water and went up on a step where I began
negotiations with a maid in German, since my
friend could not use that tongue with as much freedom as he could discuss it. The result was we
were ushered into the parlor of the Superior, who
was a lovely old lady of nearly, if not quite, eighty
years. All her life had been spent in this place,
and my friend, who had visited Jerusalem twenty-
five years before, had only to renew the acquaintance made then.

The narration of her work for the years gone by
occupied nearly all the time, which we found pass-

ing so rapidly that we had to hurry to reach the hotel in time for luncheon. But the memory of that dear old woman whose life had been one long exile, whose whole soul seemed in her work, reposing in a way after her long day of labor, was decidedly touching.

After dinner we took the opportunity to visit the Jewish schools. As they were very near our hotel, it quite naturally chanced that we deferred it until the last. Directly opposite the hotel stands the building known as the Bishop's Palace, because the former Bishop of Jerusalem had occupied it when alive. Beyond that came the English Church, its pretty Gothic architecture contrasting with the squareness of all the other structures, and still farther on, quite at the other end of the little square, of which I have before spoken, were the schools for the boys. The great amount of money contributed for this purpose of course keeps these schools in perfect order. I do not remember how large was the force of teachers and guardians, but the number of boys was, I think, not over thirty. They come from the lowest ranks, and instead of becoming Christians, I fancy they simply become hypocrites. At any rate such is the general poverty of the applicants that such a result would not be at all improbable. The boys I saw were bright and keen-looking, and make, I fancy, tolerably clever men.

The Jews of Jerusalem are, however, very degraded and miserable. The eagerness with which the English pour their money into this charity would be to my mind the strongest proof that they were the ten lost tribes. It is a standing joke in England that it costs five thousand pounds to convert a Jew. I fancy these figures are not much out of the way. However, some people say that it is not right to look upon a soul from a money standpoint.

The school for girls has only recently been established apart from the others. It is in a street on  Mount Zion which, narrow, and at times steep, threatens in wet weather to cause destruction to one's limbs. If there is anything that is uninteresting in bad weather, or in any kind of weather, it is an Eastern street. The blank walls, the rough stones, the narrow way, disputed at different points by donkeys, passersby, and camels, all tend to make up a sort of dismal effect, which is depressing in the extreme. Thus, perhaps, I was the more delighted when the door, simple and unostentatious, was opened and we found ourselves standing within the school for girls. There was more interest to me in this visit, because this school had been placed in a native house, to which another had been added to give requisite room for all the details of housekeeping. The hill of Zion here slopes quite rapidly, so this house was built with one side more open than the other. From the street, it was necessary to descend several steps to reach the main floor. Below, another story down, was a small court-yard, around which the different offices were placed. The galleries were hung with trailing plants, the doors stood open, and comfortable, cheerful interiors were seen on every side. Toward Mount Moriah, the wall of the house was not so high as to cut off the sunlight, or entirely to intercept the view. Passing through a doorway, we found ourselves in the drawing-room, which, being the home of a lady, was delightful in its simple home comforts. Thence we were taken to the other parts of the establishment, shown the various school-rooms, and examined with interest the various details of the house itself.

The visit I thus paid to a dwelling, entirely native in construction, gave me quite a longing for a house of my own, as Mr. Prime had when he visited Jerusalem. Indeed, I can fancy that a residence of a year in this place would be by no means disagreeable. In winter it is sometimes chilly, but snow does not often fall, and there are many days when the sun is bright enough to give one perfect comfort. The first of

March found doors open, rooms warmed by no fire,
plants flourishing, and a genial atmosphere. If one
could have a house on Mount Zion with a window
looking off toward the dome of Omar, with Olivet
just standing a little up above the city wall, and all
kinds of houses below, what could be more delightful !

It must seem a great pity to any one visiting the
Holy City that the English Government, or if that is
impracticable, some other, does not take Palestine, or
at least that country surrounding Jerusalem, under
its own especial protection. It is of very little value to the Turkish Government ; indeed, I fancy a
very moderate sum down would accomplish the object without difficulty. Were this once accomplished, and people could be encouraged to undertake substantial improvements to the country, the
effect would be almost miraculous. At present,
every year sees some great step forward. This has
been more conspicuous since the power of the Porte
has waned ; and, were it altogether withdrawn from
this territory, many wonderful results would follow.
If Jerusalem could be under the intelligent government of some English official, it would be in
every respect a delightful place of residence. Under proper protection, researches of the greatest importance could be made, the city would grow because of its fame, and the modern Jerusalem might
be made a splendid financial transaction.

Indeed it seems very strange to me that some of the great bankers, who have not only vast amounts of money but also influence equal to a king's, do not take this in hand. But until safety to property is guaranteed there can be no adequate results. All parties must hesitate before building largely ; and certainly under Turkish rule there can be no such thing as municipal improvements. While I am in no sense an advocate for the benefits of immi-  grant life, I do think that Jerusalem, and much of the country around, might be admirably utilized for the purpose of relieving the overcrowded condition of many of the large cities of the earth. For all seasons the climate, in the first place, is as good perhaps as can be found anywhere. It is neither too hot in summer, nor too cold in winter. Industry is repaid far better there than in most parts of the earth. Care, forethought, energy and thrift would surely bring this land back to its former state. What has been done in past time can be done again in the future. Indeed, it seems to me that the day may not be so far distant when the Jews shall return.

IX.

The Way to the Jordan.

MONDAY we started for Jericho and were obliged to be up in time to begin the day's work promptly. To my mind there was great satisfaction in leaving the refinement and comfort of cities, even if they were those of Jerusalem, to throw ourselves on the cold mercies of an Arab population. In fact I think the long tour, as it is called, is very attractive before one tries it, and also very pleasant to look back on. What it was in the meantime it shall be my duty to describe.

I had already agreed with the dragoman that I should have another horse for this trip, and should not ride the battered and shabby old hack I had ridden to Bethlehem. I went, as so many others

9

go to the East, with a profound distrust for the
Arab, and a kind of brotherly love for the European, and I returned with reversed notions, as I
think many another has before me. The sweet,
calm confidence with which I walked down the
stone steps of the hotel, out into the little alley
leading to the street, and the pleasant smile I had
on my face as I stood on the last step looking out
into the little plaza before me, excite my wonder as
I reflect upon them. With this calm trust in my
fellows I walked across the street to the place
where the horses were gathered together. My riding whip I used with a frolicsomeness which showed
my amiability, and the critical glance which I cast
around upon the assembled horseflesh, a term literally true, that is, far more descriptive than any
other I know of, was simply fatuous. But at last I
singled out the dragoman from the rest of the dark-
skinned, turbaned men, and asked him where my
horse was. He seemed a little shy, a little afraid
as it now appears to me, but after some confusion he
pointed to the most respectable horse in the number and said he thought that was the one. I was
well content.   I mounted the animal and rode him
out of the Jaffa Gate with satisfaction. I looked
his points over like an expert, and after I cantered
him, and trotted him, and walked him to my heart's
desire, I returned to the rendezvous entirely
pleased.

"He will do," I said blithely, as I dismounted and went into the hotel to finish my arrangements for the journey. The party were gathering together by this time and some were already mounted. I had nothing much to do, for my luggage had already been sent on. As I came out of the hotel I found the waiter ready, as usual in hotels, to receive a fee. This astonished me, because Cook distinctly provides for the fees, and says, a member of his party has nothing of that kind to annoy him. However, I did not let this matter trouble me ; I did not expect to see Jerusalem again in the lifetime of that waiter, and so long as I had done my duty my conscience was all right.

I came out and walked up to the horse whose merits had satisfied me and mounted him, when a man stepped up and said,

"That is Mr. C——'s horse."

This was very unpleasant, but I was determined to make a stand.

"I think you are mistaken," I said. "I just tried him by the dragoman's orders."

"Can't help that," said this man, "he is Mr. C——'s horse." Mr. C—— came up at this moment and I asked him.

"Yes," he said, "I had this horse to go to Bethlehem yesterday." There was nothing further to be done. I dismounted and sought the dragoman.

"Where is my horse ?" I demanded.

"That one there," said he, pointing to the one I had just left.

"No, that is Mr. C——'s horse." He went and consulted with the other man who was Mr. C——'s dragoman. The result was quite as might be supposed. I had no horse.

"Where is my horse ?" demanded I, after I had recovered enough of my equanimity to be calm.

"I don't know," replied the dragoman in perplexity.

"I am going to the Jordan, I suppose," I remarked a little sarcastically.

"Oh, you will have a horse," said he. Then he went and consulted with the smooth-tongued agent, and finally the latter gentleman came up to me and said, pointing to a white horse near by,

"This is your horse."

"But that is the one I rode to Bethlehem."

"Oh, no," said the oily creature, "it is not, I know it is not."

"But," I said, growing suspicious, "it looks just the same." I searched for the sore, which had so greatly enlisted my sympathies, and could not find it. I began to think I must be mistaken, so I mounted the animal, while a friend standing by remarked that it was the same horse I rode to Bethlehem, and then the agent came forward, and with the most unblushing effrontery told such an awful falsehood, that my mind still wonders.

"I know this is not the horse you rode to Bethlehem. I know this horse very well, I have ridden it myself, and it is a very easy rider, and just the horse you want. You can take my word for it." He looked so bland and innocent, and had such a kind and refined expression, that I swallowed his statements, while my friend shook his head, still in doubt. But it never occurred to me that a man who had any self-respect, could deliberately lie about that which could not have greatly concerned him. But then he was an American, and why should an American live in the uttermost part of the earth? The fact is, I am very suspicious about those people who live so far away from home. If they live and are respected where they are known, surely they would find life much better there. I accepted the situation, and rode after my party out of the Jaffa Gate, with comparative calmness. I bade farewell to Jerusalem, not perhaps with sorrow, but still with regret. I had had as enjoyable a week there as one could wish. Surely there was nothing to offend, and there was much to please. While I was leaving that, which in this short time had seemed like home, I was pressing on to that new experience, tent-life in the Holy Land. Jerusalem was like a home, and I cannot account for it, unless it is the home of the soul. The hotel was not above the average, the accommodations savored greatly of frontier life, the city itself was not beautiful, the people were uninteresting. But then there was more than this to give the place a charm. It was the center of all that is religious, all that is holy. It was the favorite central point of our Lord's ministry. All the disadvantages were naught when compared with this. So the high Tower of David was not altogether free from a certain regret in my mind, and the walls of the city, which grew higher as we descended into the valley, were not less pathetic, since there was an adieu in the air, which would be doubtless a farewell forever. Is it strange that some kind of sentiment should mingle with one's feeling at such a moment? Is Jerusalem only a show place? No; if there is aught in association, we must find it in this city. And so we went down into the valley, we went lower and lower, so that perhaps the spirits drooped accordingly, and Jerusalem gradually vanished from view, not from growing less, but from rising farther and farther up into the air as we descended, a fitting parting, for Jerusalem should always rise above us toward heaven, as a symbol of the new Jerusalem in the future.

Thus we passed the Pool of Gihon, the ancient tombs, and also, at the left, the Pool of Siloam. The journey to the Jordan was well begun for the rest of the party, but for me there was not so much pleasure. However, it was not until we got to the first khan on the road, that I discovered that my horse was the identical animal I rode to Bethlehem. When I dismounted to let him drink at this place, I saw the girths were stained with blood. Examination showed that the poor animal was really suffering from cruelty. My whole soul revolted at the sight, and the indignation of the party was aroused. The dragoman  was summoned and arraigned severely. I plainly asserted that I had been dealt with unfairly, and demanded some change. It seemed, of course, too late for this, but the dragoman at last promised to do something when we got to the Jordan. So I was obliged to rest content.

Our ride had been through a country which was sufficiently waste and barren, but it was nothing to compare with that which was before us. We were now in the midst of the Wilderness of Judea, and the deep valleys were like gorges. Such a sparse vegetation appeared along the road, that it only heightened the general misery of the place. One could not but reflect that the man who went down from Jerusalem to Jericho might, quite readily, fall among thieves. Indeed, to this day the terror of thieves is kept up, probably in order to gain money. Mr. Oliphant says that the road is as safe as any

road in a more civilized country, and, while it
might not be just the thing to go alone in the night,
that no harm would befall one in the daytime.
This statement may be true, but one cannot but
have a very insecure feeling as he rides for hours
among these high bluffs, which of themselves are
awe-inspiring by their deserted appearance, and
reflect that probably there is not a human habitation within miles. My confidence in the human
race is not so great as this, and I am perfectly
well aware that in our own well-ordered country
the man possessed of valuables passing over a plain
which was many miles from human help, would
probably be murdered before half way over. While
I have a certain confidence in the Arab race, I
have still more confidence in human nature.

At last we came to the khan where tradition
puts the inn to which the Good Samaritan brought
the wounded man, who was so rash as to try to go
this road alone. Charles Dudley Warner says he
went in and sat down to meditate upon the great
rise in hotel prices. It was an appropriate and
fitting thing to do. This way to Jericho was always
deserted and dreary, although the great thoroughfare from the capital to the rich city of the plain.
The mountainous nature of the country, with its
deep cuts, seams the whole district, and after we
had climbed the hill by Bethany we then descended
into the valley called the Wady Kelt. For a con-

siderable distance the road stretches on nearly level, although the high ground on each side still maintains the grim appearance of the wilderness. Thorny bushes, which are all too abundant in Palestine, are here numerous, and the stones which lie in the bed of the small stream show the torrents of earlier months. The silence of death reigns except when one of our party sees fit to talk loudly, or to laugh out, and then the rocks and sides of the gorge ring out in a mournful way, and their echoes, dying out suddenly, leave a sad feeling, as though some one had been frivolous at a funeral. The road, moreover, is not good, although I see Mr. Oliphant says a Wallachian princess has repaired it. I am quite of the opinion I should rather go to the Jordan on horseback, or even on foot, than attempt it in a carriage.

We must give way to some mournful reflections as we come along this deserted track. Was it down this cut David went when, old and gray-haired, he fled from his rebellious son ? Shimel could hurl stones from the top of the ravine, had he been so disposed, with perfect ease. Surely this ravine was always a little tragical for, situated in the midst of a great wilderness and at  the same time the highway between two large cities, it gave great opportunities for crime of every kind. So with these thoughts in mind, reflecting upon so much in the past, and also not a little solicitous about the present, we came to a ruined khan which also bears the traditional honor of being the scene of the Good Samaritan's charity. As the Good Samaritan was simply an illustration, one cannot help reflecting upon the morbid desire to locate things which some people have. These ruins are not old ; in fact, they are simply the ruins of some inn of no earlier date than the middle ages. How they could have lasted all . these centuries is something beyond the comprehension of one who has looked into the subject of antiquities. But they were welcome to us, for we had been riding for some weary hours, and wanted, with all the desire born of new experiences, something to eat. Besides, as we were only newly accustomed to the saddle, there was a satisfaction in rest. Thus it was with an unseemly delight, I must confess, we saw our attendant, whom we had not hitherto much regarded, bring up his horse and proceed to unload him. The place we selected for a temporary halt was a room in one of the ruins, which had walls about eight feet high and no roof. Here upon rugs spread out for us we reclined. The two Hungarians and myself formed one group. Others of the party being new to each other were more distant. The clatter of German seemed to exercise a kind of quieting effect upon the rest, and the Hungarians and myself had the conversation quite to ourselves, although the others were in no wise benefited thereby, since they could not speak the language. I was beginning to catch the Hungarian accent and to understand that "meet" was their idea of "müde."

We had no reason to be dissatisfied with our luncheon. In fact, in the wilderness we could hardly have expected so much. There were cold chicken, cold tongue, boiled ham, and boiled eggs, with plenty of fine bread and good butter. Then we had lemons with which we made lemonade, besides all sorts of condiments, pickles, and olives. A picnic appeals to most imaginations, and I feel sure that we enjoyed this our first day extremely, because it was in every sense novel and weird. After the cravings of hunger had subsided we indulged in that quiet rest which was almost a siesta, although no one went to sleep. A dreamy stillness pervaded the air, and the Hungarians offered such an advantageous model that instinctively my hands sought my sketch-book. Lying there with their heads and their bodies swathed in long pieces of white linen they presented a singular appearance. The handsome dark face of the taller, with his bright dark eyes, which had all the grace and all the beauty of the far-famed houri of the East, and the piquant countenance of the other, the livelier of the two, made an interesting group. Under circumstances so favorable it did not take me long to transfer their faces to paper.

The thought strikes me that while they were always kind, after this they were far more so. 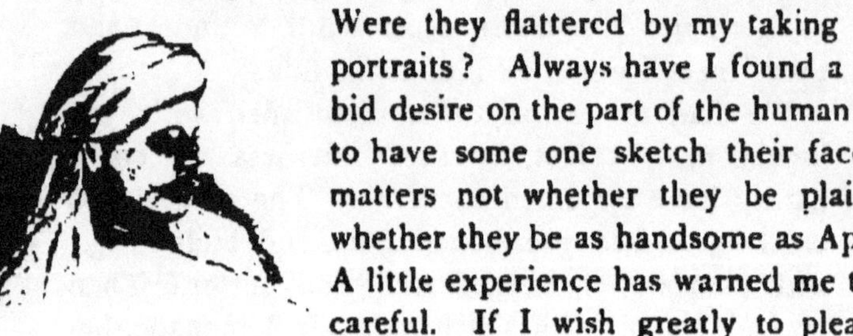 Were they flattered by my taking their portraits ? Always have I found a morbid desire on the part of the human race to have some one sketch their faces, it matters not whether they be plain or whether they be as handsome as Apollo. A little experience has warned me to be careful. If I wish greatly to please I make a fascinating picture, which has no earthly resemblance to the original, and the sitter is my friend for life. If I am careless and neglectful of my worldly interest, I simply put on paper what I see before me. Every one else recognizes the portrait ; but the man whose picture has been taken is cut to the heart, grieved beyond measure. It is a very foolish thing to take a person's picture, for he seems to think one puts on paper, not what is the actual shape of his face, but that image which the artist has in mind. In short, he looks upon a likeness which is true to life as an insult.

But the Hungarians were good-looking and I was a little fascinated with them, and perhaps, well, perhaps I did flatter them just a little. At any rate it was as good a way as any to get acquainted with them, and as I was perfectly well aware I should not see them again, I was willing to make the most of my present opportunities. The time we lingered in the old khan was all too short, and we were recalled to our horses too soon. I mounted my poor animal, for which I had at first so much pity, but which was now softening gradually into mere self-respect. Thus it is with any suffering. At first we are touched, but soon we only act according to that which we know to be proper. I mounted the horse therefore with little feeling. In fact my ride to the Jordan would have been far too miserable had I allowed myself to think of his bleeding side.

One thought as we left the khan came to the mind. As this was the undoubted route to Jerusalem from Jericho, our Lord must have rested upon this very spot. Surely such unhappiness as he felt when coming up this way the Friday before his death must touch the hardest heart.

But we are now come into the declining ravines of the wilderness, where the road descends with great rapidity, until we at last find ourselves, after treading our way along sheer precipices and over stony roads, at the opening where the first view of the Jordan plain bursts on the vision. The dark frowning aspect of the Wady Kelt gives place to a blooming country which lies open before us. On one side is a foaming torrent which is caused by the winter rains cutting down deep into the earth. This was supposed to be identical with the brook

Cherith, where Elijah hid himself and was fed by the ravens. But it is now thought that a wady on the other side of Jordan has better claims to the honor. The Jordan Valley spreads out before one like a garden, heightened in effect by the deep gash in the mountains which we have just left. The trees of the nearer distance form a great patch of pleasing color after the browns of the wady, and the hills of Moab which rise beyond are faintly  blue, giving a little distance, which has been so much cut off from our view all the way from Jerusalem. The desolation of the wilderness behind us, with its chalk cliffs, its jagged and harsh outlines, its sparse vegetation, and its solemn appearance, is changed like some magic picture, and we refuse to glance behind, as though there was some phantom with hideous shape pursuing us. The course of the Jordan, famed of rivers, the northern end of the Dead Sea, Nebo, Moab, all come crowding upon our minds in a fashion so confused that we can hardly comprehend it. Even the numerous caves of the hermits, which can be seen all around in the cliffs above us, pass unheeded, for we are more than fascinated by that which is below us. The yellow of the plain, where the mud of ages has accumulated, is even picturesque. So long has my eye been denied color, that the soft greens of the olive trees, and the still softer yellow tints are a beautiful and harmonious combination.

Below us lie several ruins, and a few small habitations, at least so they seem from the distance where we stand. We have no time to s o r t them out, and decide which is the Jericho of all, that which was conquered by the blowing of horns. Nor have we

time to think what has passed upon this great plain before us. Our time is too short, we have untried horses, and are descending a road, which would be viewed, even in America, a land of poor roads, with simple disgust. Yet we are perhaps wrong, for did not a certain princess spend ten thousand dollars in repairing it ? At last, however, we find ourselves in the " ghor," as it is called, the hollow of the Jordan, three hundred or four hundred feet below the level of the sea. We have come down three thousand feet from Jerusalem, and have still eight hundred feet to descend to reach the Dead Sea. We finally reach something like level ground, and ambitious to reach camp, the younger portion strike out for themselves, and, as we have three dragomans in the party, we cannot go wrong. We have to ford a little stream, and then we find ourselves cantering along on the edge of the fertile plain, and soon the tents are in sight.

X.

The Dead Sea and the Jordan.

WHEN we arrived at the Fountain of Elisha, or Ain es-Sultan, we had the first taste of real Oriental travel. Hitherto, we had gone, like travelers in other lands, from hotel to hotel, or from house to house, but now we were breaking loose from civilized customs, and were launching forth into a nomadic life. The sensation was pleasant, because, I think, to almost every one there is some attraction in tenting. While many of us feel the attraction, but realize the disadvantages in our own country, at any time of the year, there could be none here, so far as we could foresee. On a little rise of ground, elevated just enough to bring the whole plain of the Jordan into view, were pitched eight tents, of a size and elegance which at first took our breath away. We were a party of eleven, and were to fare sumptuously in the desert, if we were to have so many tents. As we rode up, servants took our horses, and we had only to dismount and enter our quarters, where we found our luggage already placed. An iron camp-bedstead, and all the comforts of a hotel, with Eastern rugs on the ground, did not make us dissatisfied with our lot for the present. Soon dinner was announced, and we were ushered into a large tent, in which a table, fully as well supplied with china and silver, as one will find in any hotel, met our gaze. Camp-chairs were placed around, and two waiters were in attendance. The dinner was served, and I was delighted to find that, even in the waste places of the earth, one may have the luxury found in more favored spots.

Indeed there was nothing that we could wish for. All was supplied and the food was most excellent. The old Arab cook was almost a genius in his way. A tent was devoted entirely to him and his equipment. There were, besides, seventeen servants and forty-five horses and mules. We were traveling in state and with a great deal of circumstance.

But the most beautiful part was the view which we had of the Jordan Valley, which lay below us, sloping gently down until it came to the river on the east, and the Dead Sea on the south. Olive trees dotted the plain, and luxuriant vegetation was to be seen on all sides, for this Jordan Valley is the richest land in the world, and it needs only a strong government to render it of the greatest benefit to mankind.   Now it is left to the Bedouin, who levy a sort of tribute upon travelers, and cultivate it so far as it is necessary to keep them in food.   Across the valley are seen the mountains of Moab, which rise up gradually from the river, and then go off to the east in a great table-land. Toward the south they assume a beautiful blue, and we know the Dead Sea lies just below, although not quite discerni-

ble from our standpoint.   But now the night is coming on, and there remains nothing for us to do but sit out in the open air and enjoy the delicious climate.   This Valley of the Jordan is sunk nearly a quarter of a mile below the level of the sea, and hence it never has that chill which darkness brings to other places.   The light has faded and a sort of dimness spreads over the plain, while the mountains of Moab retain a faint light from the west.   But night, like some misty cloud, has filled the Valley of the Jordan, and blotted it out from view, so that we live in a superior world which lies above.   However, we are not long left in ignorance that there is a world below, for out of the night, like the sharp note of some bird, rises that most peculiar and yet most thrilling cry of the Bedouin, which like a tremolo rings out on the clear, still air, growing shriller and shriller, but at last it dies away into silence. The feeling of awe when this is first heard is indescribable. There is something so uncanny when one reflects upon the reputation of the place, and the nature of the inhabitants, who seem in the daytime so few and so far between. But listen ; from another part of the plain comes the answer, rising, rising sharp and shrill, and then this too dies away. Then, from another part still, there rises another cry, and soon one feels as though a mighty army lies below, and we poor mortals are at its mercy. But then, perhaps, it ceases, and we hear nothing except the cry of the jackals, which are at times sufficiently near to cause the ladies a little fear. So from time to time there comes some noise, which is awesome from the intense stillness of the night. But after a little we get accustomed to this, and lie there on our rugs, or on the bags of fodder which we happen to have with us, and gaze at the stars above, which twinkle upon us and those so dear and yet so far.

The sensation of being in a strange and barbarous country like this, is one so singular that it is, for itself, worth obtaining. But then there are other features which ought to attract. When not thinking of anything, but drinking in the surroundings with fullest enjoyment, there appears, as we keep our eyes on the eastern horizon, a faint light. The mountains of Moab take an outline, and we can see clearly their irregular shape. Then as the light grows brighter we see a soft mist gather in the valley between us and the mountains. A kind of glory, quite unearthly, steals around us, and all are silent, when slowly, majestically, the golden edge of the moon shows itself above the horizon, taking shape rapidly, yet as with magic power, until it clears the land and springs forth in all its magnificent beauty up into the clouds, to sail away to regions of bliss. Never have I seen

anything equal it, never was the light so heavenly, and never did the atmosphere have so miraculous an appearance, as on this one night when we were by Jordan's shore. So the light spread over us all, through all the valley, making first one thing clear and then another, until the landscape was like some magic picture, slowly gathering shape and reality.

Then dark figures began to flit about, so that we felt a little uneasy at their presence; but we had no need to fear, for soon the dragoman, wily American that he was, said we could now witness the famous sword-dance, if we would each contribute fifty cents. We did so with reluctance for we each thought there was much fraud about the matter, and then the shadowy forms took shape, and began their dance, in which the sword played so inconspicuous a part that I must say I wonder why it was so named. The uncouth, ragged forms of the men and women, their ungainly gestures, their general air of depravity, left in our minds nothing but a feeling of disgust. Then too, as we reflected upon the matter, and learned more of our dragoman, we became assured that he had put the larger part of the money into his own pocket. Altogether it was a failure, and the cry of the Bedouin, when uttered near at hand, by a vagabond who would not be allowed on the streets of New York, reduced the romance and the terror to a very low degree.

The next morning, we started for the Jordan and the Dead Sea. I was very positive about my horse. The dragoman had promised to give me a better one, so, when the rest were already mounted, a small, pretty animal, the best-looking horse in the party, was led up for me to mount. I looked on him with pleasure, for I had ridden a good deal in my youth, and was not afraid of an ordinary animal. But I

have found, as I grow older, that one is constantly
learning. Why I should suppose that an Arab horse
was like an American horse,
I cannot tell. Yet it never
dawned upon me, in spite
of an experience I had
in Heidelberg, that there
could be any difference.
I mounted with satisfac-
tion, for I thought I had
accomplished two objects;
I had a good horse, one
that was perfectly whole,
and I also had an animal with some life. Thus
when I followed the rest of the party, it was with
considerable self-congratulation. The luncheon-
man came along on my other horse, and for a short
distance all went well. The road was down an in-
cline, leading to the more fertile part of the valley.
The trees, which I had seen from the camp, began
to appear more distinct. The bushes became
thicker as I advanced, a little doubtful by this time
whether my horse was just the kind I wished for after all. But I pursued my way with as much quiet-
ness of mind as was possible, and found it more
and more difficult, as I went along, to maintain my
mental equilibrium.

The real trouble, as I soon discovered, lay in the
fact that, while undoubtedly my horse was an ex-

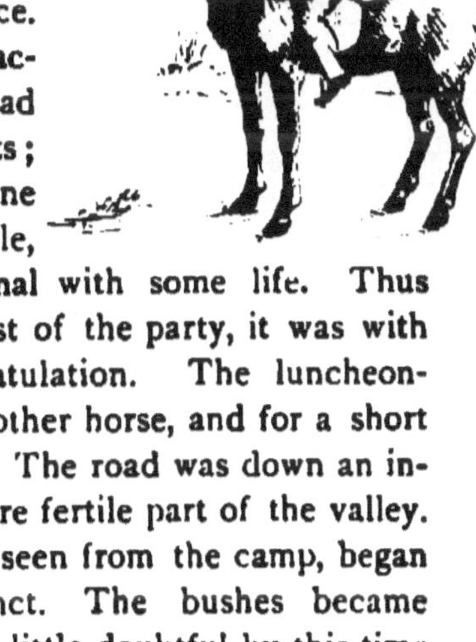

cellent animal, he had never been taught to go forward. I then learned, that Arab horses were never broken in, but were just saddled and ridden by a man who held them in by a cruel bit, and urged them forward by spurs, still more cruel. Thus, the horse found himself between two fires. I had the bit, but, unfortunately, I did not have the spurs, so the larger part of the three miles I rode the beast was consumed in taking a circular motion. He would do everything, except go straight ahead. Thus, while I covered far more ground than any of the others, I soon fell far behind them all. I need not say it was unpleasant. It is bad enough to ride a fractious horse, when one speaks the same language, but to attempt to train an Arab animal was more, I freely confess, than I was prepared to do. I was traveling for pleasure, not to drill Mr. Cook's vicious brutes, so, there being only one thing to do, I signaled to the luncheon-man, and offered to exchange. I noticed he did this with some hesitation. But as I was positive, and poured out so much bad Italian, for he was a Maltese named Luigi, he was forced to submit.

Once more seated on my old familiar steed I soon caught up with the party. I blew up the dragoman a little because he had done so poorly with his horses, but he only looked despondent, and did not see apparently any relief. Thus it happened that all through the country I was forced to ride the wounded animal I vowed I would not ride. Indeed, after the first feeling of disgust had passed off, and I saw that the horse did not mind it as much as I did, I became reconciled to him, for he was without doubt the easiest horse to ride in the whole party. From this time, however, I laid up a grudge against Cook, and wondered why it was that self-respecting people like myself were obliged to trust to his tender mercies. The Hungarians, although temporarily with our party, had their own dragoman, and had also good horses. So that it is clear that good horses are to be had, although travelers always exclaim at their badness.

But we rode through this oasis of vegetation, which forms the higher part of the valley, for it slopes gradually down until it comes to the mud formation, which was, until within a few centuries, the bed of the Jordan. Indeed it is true that the Jordan once washed the hills of the Wilderness of Judea, making a mighty river which flowed down this valley at an elevation very much higher than the present stream. But all this was of course ages ago, when this singular place was forming. Now we see mud which is left, perhaps, by the river when it is unusually high. Very little vegetation is to be seen, and sand and mud make a very nice road, over which our horses cantered as they went to the Dead Sea, only a few miles away.

As we approach this famous sea, we cannot but re-

flect upon the history of all the surrounding country.
From the time when Abraham and Lot divided the
land, all through the ages, there has been one event
after another to fascinate the mind. The burning of
the Cities of the Plain, the first recorded devastation,
was doubtless caused by the bitumen which surrounds the shores of this sea.   Indeed, wells of

petroleum abound, and, during an earthquake, ooze
up through the ground, and lightning from heaven
would easily set this afire.   The whole region is the
result of volcanic action.   The fact that the level of
the Dead Sea is nearly a quarter of a mile below the
Mediterranean, and the whole " ghor " or valley,
even beyond the Sea of Galilee, is depressed below
the surface of the ocean, bears witness to the great
disturbances which went on here in the past.   It is
conjectured that then the valley was one vast river
lying high up in the mountains, flowing during the
glacial period down through this region ; that then

the water, leaking through the earth's crust, caused volcanic action, which opened the crust, rending apart the earth, and leaving a deep hollow in course of time, which now presents the strange features we are recording. So the water which, coming down, found no outlet, gradually shrank away, until we have now about 20,000,000 cubic feet, daily, poured into this hollow, which is as rapidly removed by evaporation. Indeed, an estimate of the evaporation shows that there are 4,000,000 more cubic feet of water taken up by the sun than is poured into the sea, which would tend to prove that it is gradually drying up. But the Arabs state that the Dead Sea is now deeper than it was fifty years ago.

This vast mass of water, some of it coming through deposits of salt, pours into the lake great quantities of mineral matter, which is left there, because the sun evaporates absolutely fresh water. Thus when we came to the edge of the lake we found salt dried upon the drift-wood, but otherwise there is nothing to show that it is not the purest spring water, for the slight breeze which was blowing up from the south sent little ripples upon the beach, which sparkled in the sunlight and delighted the eyes. Vegetation grows quite near the shore, and, indeed,

in spots where fresh water is poured in, there are
oases extending quite to the water's edge. The
lake sends up no noxious odors and has plenty of
life around it, but none at all in it.

I was reminded of the sermon a friend preached
and had printed, in which he had put the most
graphic picture of the Dead Sea, with its poisonous
gases and deadly presence, and the pure limpid
waters of the Jordan pouring into this scene of filth.
Unfortunately for the sermon the illustration was
absolutely untrue. The Jordan stream is muddy
and roily, and the Dead Sea is apparently pure and
clear.

Of course the impulse of all the men was to bathe
in this singular water, which was so beautifully
transparent, yet so filled with saline matter. The
dragoman took our little party to one side, and under
the bluff about ten feet high we found a convenient
place for disrobing. The sensation of the water is a
little singular, when one gets far enough in to begin
to float. Although it is impossible to sink, it is quite
possible to lose one's equilibrium, and to get the
nostrils and mouth full of water ; then the sensation of burning is extremely unpleasant. But a little
care makes it easy to float. Thus a half hour may
be very pleasantly spent upon its placid bosom, for
it is almost impossible to get under the surface.
Still, when one is in shallow water, the buoyant qualities of the water seem almost nothing. One walks

with ease until about half under water, when suddenly the feet grow light, and the body will become inverted. As we came out, the water dried on our skin in a thick, oily substance, which, if left exposed sufficiently long, to the sun will become a fine incrustation of salt. It is not possible to get the water all off by rubbing, so that most people take a second bath, generally in the Jordan, for this purpose.

The lake stretches away in placid beauty forty-six miles to the south, and is ten miles at its widest part. On either hand rise the mountains of Moab and of Judea. Deep ravines cut into the bank, through which wadies are faintly seen, and down these defiles rush torrents during the rainy season, causing the lake to rise sometimes as high as fifteen feet. This surplus of water is rapidly carried off by evaporation, and the lake returns to its usual level. Near to the Moab shore the depth is about thirteen hundred feet, while to the south it is not more than ten feet. The scene is one of singular beauty, and not, as might be supposed by those who fancy this a sheet of noxious water, a disagreeable spot. The hills on either hand show their quaint forms, it is true, but these are so softened by the distance, as they fade away toward the south, that one does not feel the severity of their shape. The beautiful blue water shining in the sun, the reeds and tall grasses, brown or yellow, near at hand, the soft yellow sand, and a delicious atmosphere, which is perhaps unrivaled, make up a scene of beauty which should linger long in the memory. It is truly a picture, in whichever direction one may look. And so we turn away from it after there is nothing more to see, and mount our horses to take our way to the Ford of the Jordan, about three miles distant. Our course is over the mud and sand deposits of the river, through bushes, and a low brushwood which skirts the stream.

At one point we see a perfect picture. It is where the purple peak of the mountain, which the

dragoman calls Nebo, starts out from an opening in the foliage, clear and delightful, directly ahead. The yellow ground makes an exquisite base, and the trees, with their dim greens, an excellent setting, and this peak is as well mounted as any picture we have in our own sweet land. Of course there is nothing for me to do but stop and take down the forms, and saturate the eye with color, to be reproduced when we halt for luncheon. Near at hand, just in one corner, is a deep cut of the river, a branch which swerves out from the main channel, and cuts a perpendicular wall into the plain. But soon I find it necessary to follow the lead, and we come into the underbrush and small growth of trees, which surround the ford of the river.

The first sight of the Jordan, rushing with swift current, surrounded by a growth of reeds and bushes, muddy, small, and apparently insignificant, did not give me the feeling of emotion, which some writers are pleased to say were their sensations. I must state very positively that I was disappointed. I could not see the beauty of mud, that is, wet mud, and I can conceive of the Jordan in no other light. The river turns and twists in tortuous course, until one understands very well how it takes two hundred miles to cover a distance of only sixty, as it does in com-

ing from the Sea of Galilee to the Dead Sea. The banks opposite, with their varied colors, however, interested me more. A bit of the land of M o a b, red distance caused by the hill just below the mountains, and then a blue line on the horizon, made, with the bright yellow of early spring, and the greens of older foliage, a singular picture.

Jordan between was simply a muddy brook.

Yet there is enough to stimulate the imagination. There is surely enough to cause one to stop and think.   The very name of Jordan, now that I can go back into my youth and reflect upon the passage of the Israelites, does retain a few memories. They say this was the very spot where Joshua encompassed his wonderful undertaking.   Of course Rationalists make faces at a believer in this kind of trash, but somehow it seems a little unkind to destroy all of a boy's fancies.   Surely most boys

like to read about that exciting period of Jewish history, when obstacles were nothing to their conquering hosts.   Yet the Jordan to-day is very commonplace.   We find that it is hard to imagine the beautiful marble steps which, we are told, led down to the place where our Lord was supposed to be baptized.   Around we have a jungle now, wild beasts are supposed to haunt its recesses, and sometimes the river rises and drives them out in terror.   Through this flood, not so very wide, but sufficiently swift, the lion-faced men of Gad swam to seek their hero David.

But then near here great crowds came to hear the preaching of John Baptist, whose severe denunciation of sin attracted the people then, as such preaching does now. It is strange how people, who will remain in their sins, love to hear them abused. It is strange how they will turn away from the man who soothes them and puts them to sleep, and seek some one who will only make them uncomfortable. Of course there may be a possibility that they will turn away from their sins and be saved, although the history of poor John Baptist, surely, is not a glorious one from a worldly standpoint. But if, among those crowds who came from idle curiosity, there came One to be baptized by John, truly this is hallowed ground. Yes, even the insignificance of the river somehow sweeps down stream, and, as one sits on the bank and looks at the chalk cliff opposite, there is a kind of mythical glory about the place, entirely in our imagination, but then really there to a devoted Christian. To this day great crowds come here at Easter-tide to be baptized. It seems pilgrims go into the water in linen garments, which are afterward used as shrouds. I like the idea. Among these old-fashioned religions occasionally one finds a good and sensible custom. I must avow my dislike of the custom people have of

11

taking Jordan water home for baptismal purposes.
In the first place, it is so dirty that until it has well
settled it is not fit.   Then after it has cleared it
is hardly Jordan water, since mud is its especial
characteristic.   To be baptized in Jordan water
strikes me as being a little superstitious.   But this
linen garment, in which one is baptized, would serve
very appropriately to cover the remains of the person after death.

Thus we came to the luncheon with perhaps as
little appetite as one would care to have.   But the
inviting results of Luigi's hands were tempting, and
for awhile we forgot our meditations and were
brought back to every-day life.   While at the Dead
Sea we fell in with an Englishman who was taking
photographs all by himself, that is, unattended except by his Bedouin escort.   It seems so singular to
see a European all alone in the wildest part of the
country.   Although it is doubtless safe, still there
must be considerable courage necessary to do it.   He
came up about the time we were taking our luncheon, and accepted an invitation to sit down with
us.

As we were sitting around, divided into little
groups of three or four, I could not but reflect upon
the strangeness of our surroundings.   The short underbrush formed walls on every side, and the young
trees which had started up in vigorous growth gave
us shade.   A little verdure here and there formed a

carpet. The Jordan sped on its way in haste, as though intent upon a good mission, only too soon to waste itself in the stagnant waters of the Dead Sea. Surely many a life is just as busy, just as eager to reach its goal, only to find at the end a cesspool, attractive no doubt to look upon, but in fact only the accumulation of centuries of false ambition.

Even if we had not been aware that we were near the historic stream, there was enough about us, yea, more than enough to gratify the senses. As usual I was with the Hungarians, who, being foreign both by language and by nationality, did not associate with the rest of the party. Attended by their dragoman, who was in every respect a faithful servant (I wish I could think of his name so as to recommend him), we were treated like princes. After we had satisfied our appetites he made delicious coffee, and served it to us in little cups no larger than an egg-shell. This Arabian coffee is very nice, after one becomes accustomed to it. The black coffee, which people serve after dinner, and which a false civilization forces upon people who are not fond of it, is simply slops compared to it. Going upon the theory that coffee must be drunk without milk, we have it made in the same manner as if to be drunk with milk, and then people decide that it is good. But it is all a mistake. One taste of Arab coffee will at once dispel the illusion.

To the Arab, coffee is not a beverage but a sweet-meat. They prepare it by grinding the berry very fine, and then, mixing it with sugar according to a certain rule, put in very little water. When this is once boiled up they dip it out, grounds and all, into the little cups, which are more than half full of grounds when presented to the guest. The correct thing is to eat it, not drink it. After a little experience one becomes very much in love with it, and for a time we indulged in this delightful dissipation, until at last I began to feel as though the top of my head would fly up into the air. At first I could not understand what was the cause, but after a little reflection I decided it must be the effects of the coffee. After that I was wary and avoided the subtle fiend.

I had a desire to bathe in the Jordan, in spite of its swift current and muddy appearance. The larger part of our number did not feel equal to its dangers, nor would I, had I a realizing sense of the undertaking. So with the Hungarians, and attended by one of the Bedouin guides, we sought the shore where there seemed the best chance of attaining our object. It looked rather formidable, but I was determined; so I ventured in, protected, and I might as well say saved, by a rope which the Bedouin had tied to my arm. He grinned good-naturedly, in fact his face was the most amiable of any I have seen, as he saw me descend into the water. I fondly hoped to find bottom somewhere, but sank into the mud for three feet, and would have been entirely submerged had I not had the good sense to come out and dress myself without washing off all of the mud I had acquired. I was fully satisfied. The Jordan no longer had any charm for me, in spite of its history, and I mounted my horse and rode after the party across the plain. For some distance it was perfectly level, and we had a merry canter. We tried our horses at racing, but soon found that the steeds of the East are not fitted for that amusement. The sun came down pretty hot, for even in winter it is very warm here, and in summer it is unbearable. Mr. Oliphant suggests, and, indeed, sees at present a disposition among the Russians to make this a winter resort. If there were a railway to Jerusalem, or even a good road from Jerusalem to the Jordan, it might easily be accomplished. In this valley or "ghor" there is a truly tropical climate, perhaps the best place for invalids within easy reach of Europe. I fancy it is not at all improbable that some day in the near future sees this transformation. Indeed, there are already twelve houses erected and a hotel. The government proposes to bridge the Jordan, and thus throw open the great country to the east. But when the government intends to do anything in this region, I prefer to see it done before I place much faith in it.

With a civilization which would make all this valley secure beyond a doubt and bring it under cultivation, a great change would be produced. Great tracts of land, extremely fertile and well watered, would yield vast quantities of sugar-cane or other produce, and, could the Turkish Government once be made to keep its pledges, some one would have a vast fortune ready made. Petroleum, bitumen, and other products are simply to be taken. Indeed, the thought of what this region might be leads us to think what it has been. When the spies came into the country from the land of Moab, they found this region flourishing with all the luxuriousness of the tropics. Indeed, Egypt was not so splendid, and the wilderness they left behind was a bleak desert. It is not strange that their report was as favorable as we read it to be. Jericho was, doubtless, situated where our camp was pitched, a city not large, if the ark went around it seven times in one day, but one of many cities which dotted the plain. Houses were on the wall with windows projecting over, and from these the spies could easily escape to the ravines near at hand and hide themselves. But this city was destroyed and rebuilt, as seems probable, many times. The second city, that of Herod, was, doubtless, at the foot of the Wady Kelt, where Herod built his gorgeous palaces, and erected back on the hills the fortress of Kypros to protect them. Josephus tells us the whole region was flourishing, covered with gardens, and the center of a rich and prosperous population. Here in this Jericho Herod died in terrible agony, expiring with a cruel command to Salome to kill the leading men of the Jews, so that some one should lament his death. But she wisely left the command unfulfilled. A few years later the great palace was burnt down, and was afterward restored in still greater splendor by his son Archelaus. This was the city where our Lord was entertained by Zacchæus, and where he healed the blind man.

The third city, the present Eriha, through which we rode on our way to the camp, is as different from the Jericho of Herod as it well can be. No fouler or viler place can be found in Palestine. Rude huts, whose walls of stone and roofs of earth are half in ruins, stand in very irregular fashion, so that unless one is particular it is sometimes difficult to distinguish between the earth and the dwellings.

The population squat around in listless fashion, more inert and shiftless, perhaps, than any of their neighbors. A little of the surrounding land is cultivated, just enough to keep the life in their wretched bodies, and they live there in a state as bad as that of the inhabitants of Sodom and Gomorrah.

When one thinks how little effort is here needed

to secure wealth, it seems pitiable to see such
squalor. Around the village is a hedge of thorns,
and a solitary palm tree marks the place.

We rode through, being far in advance of our
party, which, consisting of several ladies and men
who were unused to the saddle, went more slowly,
and soon we found ourselves off the road which led
to the camp. However, it did not so much matter,
for with the landmarks around so conspicuous it
was impossible to get lost. But we soon saw our
destination plainly before us, and hastened into
camp to end the day by a chat with each other
upon the things we had seen.

This was the last night with the Hungarians, for
they were to return to Jerusalem on the morrow
with their dragoman, while we were to ascend the
steeper hill to Bethel. I felt the parting more than
usual, for few travelers become attached to their
companions as I had become attached to these
young men. In all their intercourse with me there
had been nothing but the most perfect courtesy,
marked by that politeness which we see in this
country extended only toward women. Even if the
foreigners do not mean their attentions, there is
something, surely, so delightful in their kindness
that the best qualities of the human being show
themselves, and one will certainly in this manner
make more friends and appear to greater advantage,
than under the system pursued by most Americans

and Englishmen. While my acquaintance with these young men had been, it is true, very slight and for a very short period of time, still there was a warmth of regard between us which could not have arisen between Americans even after months of companionship. Why should one display all his faults ? · Why not appear to be kind if one is really not ?

The rest of the day was greatly tinctured by regret that we must part. I urged them to go through the country, they that I should return to Jerusalem with them. But it was impossible, and, although they begged me to visit them in Buda-Pesth, I was perfectly well aware that our parting was to be final. I heard of them afterward, for they went to Constantinople with my former companions. The handsomer of the two evidently fell deeply in love with the bright girl from Boston. She attempted to teach him English with the following results. She tried to make him say that " Mary had a little lamb." He replied :

" Mary had lit'lum."

" No, ' Mary had a little lamb.' "

Mary hadie lit'lum."

" No, no," cried the sweet creature, no doubt enjoying her teaching, "you must say, ' Mary had a little lamb.' "

" Mary had a—I love you, Mees Mabel," was the reply. And so through all that journey his dark eyes must have flashed that answer into her face, an answer which she did not altogether dislike, I fancy, if I knew her at all well. Indeed, there must have been a great deal of fun among the party, for all the conversation which they could have between them lay through the scanty French of the Hungarians and the none too perfect knowledge of that tongue by the Americans. This was the last I heard of these very interesting young men, and it has always been a matter of regret to me that I did not face the difficulties and return home by way of Varna and Vienna.

About five o'clock in the afternoon the sun was

going down a little behind the mountains in the rear of our camp. The tents were open, and around were spread rugs and sacks of fodder for the animals. Not far off were the servants sitting down in a circle, carrying on some kind of a conversation in their guttural language. At the doors of the tents lounged the Hungarians, myself, and the young men of the party. The tent of the cook was opened toward the east, and a savory smell began to arise from his quarters. Insensibly we seated ourselves around him, as he became more and more absorbed in his preparations, for we were interested to know how it was possible for a man, who had to pack everything each day, to bring forth such savory dishes. Far off to the east stretched the plain, no longer unknown, and thus better appreciated by us. The glistening sea we knew lay just out of sight, and the blue hills beyond were far on the eastern coast. To dream was the order of the day. The warmth remaining in the air, now that the sun had hid itself a little, induced a sweet languor. We were resting before the hardships of the journey, and I feel sure there were few who would not have wished to remain in this spot, so favored by nature, a little longer.

After the dinner, which came as the darkness was growing deeper, we returned to our lounging places, well content to enjoy as much as was possible of this air which so deliciously fanned our cheeks. Even after the moon had risen, and we had examined the little camp of our Bedouin attendants, we were content to listen to the night-cries which were now somewhat older, although still interesting. And so, at last, as the journey the next day was to be severe and trying to our unaccustomed natures, we retired early to sleep the sleep of the just. Alone in the wilderness !   It was a strange feeling, yet was there not enough to protect us in the thought that here our Lord was wont to come ?   This place, sanctified by his presence, should surely only require the perfect trust in him to make it secure to us.

XI.

Climbing to Bethel.

WE arose the next morning with a chill. There had been a great deal of moisture in the air, and the heat of the day before had all passed away. The sun had hardly asserted itself through the haze which had gathered in the night, and we were, moreover, sleepy and ill-disposed to undertake the hardships of climbing the hill on our way to Bethel. Indeed, it is hard to turn away from that which is luxurious and beautiful, to face the rugged paths of the desert.

At breakfast each looked cross; even the Hungarians, who, while quite polite, did not seem so merry as they had the night previous. Evidently this was a blue day. If it had been Monday we could have borne it, but it was now Wednesday, and we had some hard traveling before us to reach Nazareth, where we intended to pass the following

Sunday.   Even the servants were cross and disagreeable, perhaps dreading the prosaic business of breaking camp.   But it must be done, and we must start early in order to reach Bethel by lunch time.

So far as I was concerned, packing up my chattels was the most disagreeable task of the whole journey.   I felt disposed to throw them all away, and go as unincumbered as the two Englishmen who once went on a Cook's tour up the Rhine.   The party was to be absent from England two months, and when the conductor asked for their luggage each held up an umbrella.   Indeed, although it seems a little shocking at first, I am not sure that they were not more sensible than the average English traveler, who takes nearly all his wardrobe and part of his household furniture with him.

Breakfast was soon dispatched, and the first duty for me was to see the Hungarians off.   The horse of the smaller of the two was very stiff, probably from exposure to the night air.   It seemed as though he would hardly reach Jerusalem.   A few farewells, and all was over.   They rode away and I returned to my own affairs, which, to be sure, were not very many.   As soon as we could get our people together, the dragoman winded his horn and we started.   The procession wound around the base of the mountain, passing into the valley of the Duk Fountain, which flows in considerable volume to the north of the Fountain of Elisha.   As we rounded a small elevation which backed our camp, we saw Quarantania directly before us, rising high and steep from out the valley, presenting its white and naked sides to view. Its summit is crowned by a little chapel, and all around it is dotted by the dark openings of the caves and cells inhabited by hermits, in vast numbers in past time, and by a few at present. Along one side runs a dark line, which is a pathway cut into the rock. One traveler describes his experience in traversing this narrow road, and his sensations in meeting a ferocious man whom it was impossible to pass. The man turned out to be harm-

less and all was well. I had no sickly sentiment about exploring places so dangerous. The view from the road below was enough for me.

The fact that tradition makes this the scene of our Lord's temptation explains why, even to this day, it is so revered by members of the Greek and Roman Churches. As such it is interesting. So with this above us and the stream rushing on below us, we find ourselves on the edge of a luxuriant vegetation. The bareness of the mountain, which seems well nigh perpendicular, throws this richness into high relief, and so our journey for a short distance is pleasant in the extreme. But this does not

last long.   We soon find we are in the very recesses
of the wilderness, and abrupt precipices on one hand
either terrify us by their depth or on the other awe
us by their height.   The road begins to ascend in
no very gentle fashion, and stones, which seemed
sufficiently abundant on our journey from Jerusalem, are far more numerous and far more troublesome here.   But the horses, whose chief concern it
is, do not appear to mind the difficulty, and so we
gradually rise until we can look back upon the Jordan plain, now visible for the first time since we left
camp.   The low hills are so far below as to hide no
longer the view, and it is with a feeling akin to sadness that we press forward, leaving behind as picturesque a view as one can find in Palestine.   The
very ruggedness of the present road and the bareness
of the ground, which seems parched, make the retro-
spect charming.   The Dead Sea glistens in the sun,
the Jordan shows a little of its yellow surface, the
green foliage of its banks, bright and fresh, and the
olive trees of the plain all stand out into prominence.

But as we go forward the road becomes worse
and the stones still more trying.   When it seems as
though no more hills could be ascended, still there
is some other elevation before us.   It is a great strain
upon our patience and energy, and withal it is a
lonely and unsatisfactory ride.   Misery of the worst
kind is all around, even the thorn tree and the
thistle seem absent.

So, as there was nothing but this same uninteresting country, we rode on until, gaining the top of a hill we saw in the distance, just beyond a shallow valley, a number of huts built against the side of the hill opposite. Quite at the top of the hill was a building of stone with a dome which I took to be a mosque. Otherwise the picture was simply brown earth, all dark, forbidding and barren. The only relief was where the brown came into contact with the blue sky, and barren as it looked, my sketch was copied by three of the party, because, as they said in explanation, it looked like the place. Near at hand was Ai, the city conquered by Joshua, placed far up from the plain, the scene of his earlier conquests.

The valley was soon traversed, and after a journey of six hours we rode into some old ruins still standing at the foot of the village, which, with its mud huts, is farther up the hill. We found an Englishman and his wife who had come up from Jerusalem waiting here to join our party and go through the country. A large palanquin had also been sent up for the use of a lady, who had been to the Jordan, in case she should not feel able to go through on horseback. The meeting was in a sense pleasant,

for we had been away from civilization just long
enough to wish to see some one whom we knew. So
sitting down in friendly fashion I began to get acquainted with the people who were to accompany
us for the next three weeks.

We had the same bill of fare which we had had for
two days past, but it was not yet worn out.   And

we arose from our siesta refreshed and cheered by
the prospect of having only a short and an easy ride
to the tents.   Meanwhile there was much reading up
in the guide-books as to the respective merits of
Bethel.   But they were entirely confined to the past ;
for at present there is nothing but squalor in the town,
and utter desolation around it. They say that at the
beginning of this century there was no habitation
here.   I must censure the bad taste of any Arab
who was so foolish as to make it his home.   Perhaps there may be some attraction in the fact that

Jacob laid his head here upon a stone, a thing so easy to do, and so impossible to avoid. From his exclamation, " this is none other than the house of God," comes its name Beth-el. Here arose a city belonging to Benjamin. Here Jeroboam raised a temple to rival the one at Jerusalem. Afterward it passed into idolatry, and its name was changed to Bethaven, "the house of idols." As a border fortress between the two kingdoms it had great importance, and is often mentioned in the Bible. Shechem alone is referred to before Bethel, and after Shechem it was the greatest sanctuary of the nation.

As we leave Bethel we ascend a ridge to the west of the village, and going down a hill strike into the road leading to the north. The way leads through a valley, which, after an hour, grows very beautiful, for around are green grass and fig trees, while terraced hills lie on every side, a vivid contrast to the desolation we have experienced since we left Ain es-Sultan. The road is not to be thought as good as the country. Indeed, quite the reverse. It is a fixed idea among the Arabs that a road is simply a place in which to throw things, so that it is possible ofttimes to find it only by observing where there are the most stones. And so we pass through the village Yebrūd, which is surrounded by vineyards and orchards, although the rocks still protrude in many places, and the wonderful richness of the soil hides this barrenness only in summer.

Passing across a plateau we soon descend into a
narrow valley, which is one of the most picturesque spots I have ever seen. A rippling brook
goes by with gentle murmur, while at the sides rise
the cliffs, partly covered with trees growing by the
side of the road, and partly with hanging plants.
We soon come to a fascinating part of the valley
where it becomes quite narrow, called the Robber's
Fountain. The water trickles down the precipice,
while the rich green grass is extremely refreshing.
It is growing dark as we reach this spot, the usual
place of encampment, but we are still to press on to
reach Sinjil, where the tents have been ordered to
be put up. This narrow gorge has borne an evil
reputation, because here robbers from neighboring
villages found it convenient to pursue their calling.
Indeed, the retired character of the place, shut in as
it is by the trees growing so luxuriantly, makes it especially adapted to dark deeds. An awesome silence
reigns around us, for no human habitation is in sight
and the ruins of a crusading fort on the bank add
to the weirdness of the scene.

From the fountain the road winds up the glen and
gradually widens. The country seems more prosperous and fertile, and a different kind of landscape
opens before us. The soft tints of early spring begin
to appear, and the declining sun is rapidly shutting
out the light, so that we are ready to seek the shelter
of our tents, for after the sun goes down there is such

a chill in the atmosphere that we need our heavy coats. Ascending a hill we come to a village of rude huts, more decent than any we have yet seen. The tents are already pitched, for we have come a long and tedious ride, while the servants, cutting across the country in a way known best to themselves, have avoided the longer route. We have earned our rest and our dinner, and never did the skill of the old Arab, who catered to our inner man, seem greater than on this one night, when seated around a bountiful board we laughed and chatted. For we had now broken through the ice of first acquaintance, and, like people at sea, were forced to be agreeable to each other. But we were not willing to remain long at the table, for we were too tired and too exhausted even to be polite for any length of time.

XII.

On to Nablous.

THE next morning we saw that the character of the country had entirely changed.   Just across the road was the village which we had dimly seen as we rode into camp, the night before, while off to the north stretched a plain somewhat diversified by rolling hills.   The country seemed fertile, at least in contrast to the barren parts we had recently left. The dragoman was growling because forced to keep watch all night, since he found it impossible to hire men from the village to perform that office.   I was surprised to learn that it was necessary, as I esteemed the country between Jerusalem and Nazareth quite safe.   But he muttered something about their picking up things if we did not look after them, and the thievish propensities of the natives, until for a short period I really began to think them as bad as he stated.

When we came out from breakfast we had the singular sensation of finding all the tents struck, packed, and already on their way to our next halting ground. Only a few mules remained to take the dinner tent and its accessories, and a sort of homesickness came over me. I felt almost as though we were some traveling circus and that we exhibited only one night in a place. Such is the expedition of the servants, which is indeed necessary in order to be ready for the travelers when they reach camp, that they make no false motions, but work with a will. Their dexterity is only equaled by the circus men in our own country. For it is no small task to strike eight tents, each one of good size, and pack them for a journey of twenty miles.

One feels upon such occasions as though there was nothing left but one's horse and Luigi, who is to look after our mid-day welfare. Here I first noticed that Luigi had a new horse, and at once demanded the reason. I found that he would not ride the vicious little beast any further and it had consequently been sent back to Jerusalem. The thought came to me that if I had been sufficiently disagreeable I might have had a new horse, and mine could have been sent back also. However, I was now becoming a little hard-hearted. In fact, one does occasionally, and as I was guaranteed a horse I did not think it so very cruel to kill one or two in going through the country. I fancy death, if it did not come in too painful a manner, would be a decided relief to these poor jaded creatures. Luigi looked a little glum and swore a little, I fear, in his native Maltese, when I remarked that the other horse was a brute. Luigi was a curious fellow, so shiftless, yet withal kind-hearted. I should not have hesitated to trust him with my life, for he appeared one of those good-natured men who are so easily controlled. Poor Luigi, I felt rather sorry for him ! In a strange land, cast about by every tide

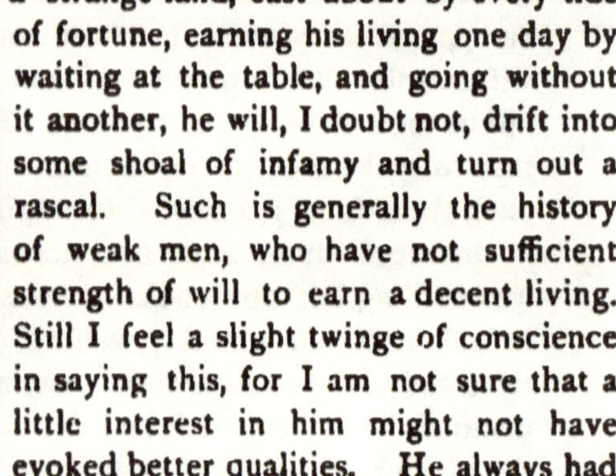

of fortune, earning his living one day by waiting at the table, and going without it another, he will, I doubt not, drift into some shoal of infamy and turn out a rascal. Such is generally the history of weak men, who have not sufficient strength of will to earn a decent living. Still I feel a slight twinge of conscience in saying this, for I am not sure that a little interest in him might not have evoked better qualities. He always had so much regard for me, waiting on me with perfect attention, seeing my wants almost before I was myself aware of them, that I felt as though a little instruction, together with a kindly interest, might have won his heart, and would not have been amiss.

Poor Luigi ! Every journey has some regrets, and I fancy that if I have any they are connected with you. Of all our attendants none came so near moving my heart with some little feeling of affection. Surely the dragoman, Leighton, who was, I must confess, kind, although such a rank impostor that even my self-respect in the matter of likes and dislikes rebelled, had no permanent place. But Luigi, with his plaintive eyes half closed, as though fate had been too much for him, and life was some hideous phantom, was too impressive. But then Luigi was not nearly so efficient as the other waiter, a full-blooded Arab, whose bright eyes were everywhere, but whose heart was nowhere. However, it made no difference. I had no fault to find with either; both were assiduous, but Luigi impressed me, and the other did not.

I do not think any of us had any real sense of what we were going to see. Even one who has been a fair Biblical student, finds upon going through the country that Jerusalem, Nazareth, and a few other points constitute his whole knowledge of the country. Besides, to his mind these places stand out in such prominence that when he sees others quite as conspicuous he is a little dazed. If one studied the country with that thoroughness with which Dr. Geikie had before he wrote the *Life of Christ*, then every stone would have a meaning. It seems Dr. Geikie had never been to the East until just after I made my trip. He went from Jaffa down to Gaza, and left us to go up to Jerusalem. He came after our party, so that when we arrived at

Beirût we heard of his being then on his way.   Such
is the accuracy of his description of Palestine in his
Life of Christ that a prominent English bishop
wrote to him, congratulating him upon his minute
and thorough search of Biblical places.   Indeed,
while this seems a little amusing, I take up the
Life of Christ to-day as the best and most picturesque description of the country I have ever read.
The later book of the doctor's, written after he saw
the country, cannot compare with it in this respect,
which, if it is faint praise, is at the same time a great
compliment to the Doctor's power of conception
when he wrote the first.   Indeed, when the Doctor
finally went through this country it was under great
affliction.   How he had the heart to write anything
seems strange.

When we started from camp we little expected, as
we turned to the right and found ourselves on an

elevation standing be-
fore some ruins, to be
told this was Shiloh.
Sacred name, which
has meant sanctuary
for so many centuries,
the place where the
Tabernacle   stood !
where Eli and Sam-
uel lived, where the
poor old high-priest fell back when he heard that

his sons were dead ! Strange people were those Israelites, governed only by their religion, yet not going so far from the laws of God as we might have expected ! Then, too, here the dance of the people was held when the sons of Benjamin carried off their wives, each seizing a damsel and hurrying off with her, in spite of her protests. Dr. Geikie suggests that perhaps some of them were not loath to thus find homes of their own. But it takes off a little of the romance of sacred history to suppose that the rage for matrimony was even then so great. This little incident brings up to mind why the Benjamites had to resort to this means of getting wives. In fact, the whole story is not dissimilar from that of the early times in Rome. Thus does history repeat itself. When the Levite who had been so hardly used at Gibeah cut up the body of his wife and sent her to the different tribes, one sees that Israel was truly a barbarous people. Then, too, the terrible revenge which was wreaked on the poor Benjamites was blood-thirsty in the extreme.

To-day there remains only a low wall built of large stones, evidently very ancient. A doorway is in the center, and the stump of an old tree stands beside the ruin. This was all that was left. The hand of time has obliterated the past, and while it is pleasant to conjecture that, perhaps, the tabernacle was erected on this ruin, still it is hardly probable. So that it is scarcely worth one's time to linger long in this place. It has naught but the memories of those early ages when the severe prophet Samuel

ruled the people and yielded, finally, to their childish whim that they should have a king.

The country is cultivated around here, and we pass through the fields, which lie on the sides of low hills or in the shallow valleys. The wild flowers of the Holy Land now begin to appear. On every side are seen the red tinges of the anemone or the thick clusters of the cyclamen. Other flowers abound, but none seem so prevalent as the two mentioned. At Sawlieh we stand on the border of Samaria. Here a ruined khan demonstrates the hatred of the Jews, who would not sleep on the soil of their enemies if it were possible to avoid it. Thus, on the extreme edge of Judea they built a resting place, so that the pious hater might have a chance to vent his harmless spite against his neighbor by traversing his country in the day time.

Climbing a steep hill, we see before us the mountains Ebal and Gerizim and the Plain of El-Mukhna near at hand. So we are content to pause and take in the scene before us. We have noticed the improvement of the country all the way thus far, but now we can gain some idea of the richness of this section. Before us lies a plain at least seven miles long and nearly two in breadth. Its surface is as smooth as though rolled for a lawn, and the soft green of the spring takes off the barren brown which has hitherto so disfigured the landscape. High to the left rise the western hills,  culminating in Ebal and Gerizim, while to the east the hills are much lower, but between them the valley seems like a basin, laid out here to catch the bounties of nature, and to bless its Creator by its fruitful increase.

While we were wondering at the scene before us, suddenly a star, as it seems, strikes our vision. Is it some signal beckoning us on to explore the north country ? Bright and shining, like some huge diamond—we hardly dare to gaze long for fear it will vanish—it stands there glittering between the northern hills. Almost awe-struck, we ask the dragoman what it means, for even if we came for nothing else, this greeting from the heavens would be enough to compensate us for all the hardships we had thus far taken.

"That," says the dragoman, " is Hermon."

Ah ! yes, it was Hermon standing high above all the hills of the Holy Land, and sending down its dew upon the mountains of Zion. The sun is shining upon its icy surface, and we are getting the brilliant reflection of its rays. It is enough. The omen is a good one. We can proceed with courage, for the welcome of Hermon that beautiful morning was all we needed. So we go down into the valley, where the road becomes good for the first time since we left Jerusalem, unless we may except a short distance on the Plain of the Jordan. Two roads lead to Nablous, which lies just in the valley between Ebal and Gerizim. We took the one leading down into the valley, for we were to stop at Jacob's Well for our luncheon. The smooth road in which, almost strange to say, there were few stones, gave the younger members of the party a chance to ride a little faster than the walk, which the timidity of a certain lady in the party had imposed upon us. The ground had been prepared for the spring crops, that is, it had just been scratched, which seems to be the Arab idea of plowing. Near here are the tombs of the family of Aaron. About three miles farther on we came to the opening of the valley between the mountains, where the ruins surrounding Jacob's Well are seen. There were in the first detachment as we rode up a Presbyterian clergyman from Pennsylvania, a young Englishman, who evidently looked upon these sacred places in the light of a lark, being in no wise impressed with them ; another young Englishman, Mr. C——, who was ultra-religious, but very unused to horses, and myself. Mr. C——'s dragoman guided us aright, and we dismounted, and explored the ruins before the rest of the party came up. There is little to be seen, but a great deal to think of. This fact was impressed so strongly upon our minds by the Englishman, who had joined us at Bethel, that we were ofttimes fain to avoid religious thoughts. His wife was a devoted creature, whose dresses must have been made in some antediluvian period, but whose mind had been treasured with all kinds of Biblical lore. The husband was equally religious, but not over-bright. In fact, I think they were traveling abroad for his health; if I added his sanity, perhaps I should be nearer correct. However, we did not learn until the end of our journey that his mind had been seriously threatened, or we might have had more charity. It did not matter what he saw, he was loud in his expressions of admiration. Even the barren slope of a hill, which showed no fertility at all and nothing but desolation, to him was a wonder of beauty.

Withal he sketched, as every Englishman does; I am sure I am right, for nearly every one I ever met did sketch or tried to sketch,

and when he sat down with a note-book not over
four inches long and two wide, and endeavored to
bring in all the plain before us, I simply put my
book into my pocket, discouraged by such evident
zeal and conscious ability. As I was very curious
to see what result he would bring forth, I remained
near him until he had finished, and in my most
deferential and polished tone asked to see it. He
surrendered it gracefully, and to this day the sketch
lingers in my memory, and will continue to do so,
until all recollection of the place itself has passed
away.

The fact that the authenticity of Jacob's Well has
never been doubted adds much to the interest of the
place. Here without doubt our Savior sat. Here
He talked to the woman of Sychar about the living
water, astonishing her, as many another since her
time, by His words. As He sat here looking over the
fertile country before Him, beautiful now, but doubtless far more beautiful then, what could have been
His thoughts? Gerizim stood near Him ; He refers
to it as " this mountain." There is much in such association. The well itself is a shaft cut into the living
rock, about nine feet in diameter and upward of
seventy feet in depth. It is now filled with rubbish,
so that probably it was once much deeper. The first
engineer doubtless intended it for a reservoir rather
than as a means of reaching a spring. All is now deserted except by the traveler, who seeks here for that

association which shall bring him near to the life of his Savior. Jacob and Abraham, with all the rest who made this the central point of their lives, are too far back in the mists of the past, and thus lose their prominence, because our Lord has brought the place so much fame by His simple and touching talk with the woman of Samaria.

We had a little hard work before us on our way to Nablous, which is the name of the present city of Shechem. So sitting down among the ruins we once more partook of cold chicken, which, delightful enough occasionally, was becoming a little tiresome.

The ride for the next two hours was up the steep sides of Gerizim, which had been a short time before just over our heads. Rising out from the plain its sides seem almost perpendicular. The way leads around by the western slope over stony roads, which seemed at one time almost impassable. But to the Arab horse there seems to be no such word as "can't," for, shod with a plate of iron, the foot is amply protected from the roughness of the way, and long experience has no doubt given it an expertness which enables it to overcome all difficulties. We should perhaps have had more mercy on our beasts, but I am sure the thought that Cook would put upon us many hardships caused us to obtain our revenge by making his animals do their full share of work. So after a while, when we have reached the other side of

13

the mountain, we emerge into a wady, where we soon come to a square inclosure, the first of the ruins. Here are the bones of the Paschal lambs which are sacrificed every year. Beyond this are the ruins of a castle and a church. The ruins show that the buildings were once of great extent, and to raise such buildings at so great a distance from the plain

was doubtless a vast undertaking. This mountain is the sacred place of the Samaritan religion. Here they come every year to practice their rites. The narration of the events is of great interest, but hardly necessary in this place. Dean Stanley thought that there was every probability that here Abraham offered up Isaac, and not at Jerusalem, and that here he met Melchizedek.

But the most beautiful feature of the place is only to be seen by mounting the walls, which still stand to the height of several feet. From this position a most glorious view presents itself on every side. Just across the valley is the Mount of Cursing, Ebal, rising even higher than Gerizim, while to the east lies out before us the valley we have just explored, closed in by the hills between it and the Jordan. Then beyond is the deep cut made by that river sinking down out of sight, while blue in the distance lies Gilead. Surely this is beautiful, even if Hermon is partly obscured by Ebal! But, when one turns to look the other way toward the sea, he is struck with surprise, for far away stretches cerulean blue extending high into the sky, until it seems as though nature has some way inverted itself. The sharp line of the horizon is so far above where our experience has told us it should be, that we cannot, for the time, understand this phenomenon. But soon it dawns upon us that we are raised three thousand feet into the air, and the farther we go up the more can we see off into that blue space, the Mediterranean. When the eye falls to the coast it seems almost under our feet. With its yellow sand-banks running along north and south the intervening space is almost insignificant. Yonder to the south is Jaffa, while this level country between is Sharon. The hills of Judea fade away into nothingness, while to the north are the outlying slopes of Mount Carmel. Surely it is all too glorious, yet, somehow, the soul shrinks within itself at gazing, for here from this one point can be seen nearly all the country, which seems to us so great and so important, when we read of it in Sacred Writ. As one might stand on the Kaaterskill and look off from its height up and down the valley of the Hudson, and think therein lay all the history of our own country, so does the idea of the Holy Land shrink within itself as we gaze. It is impossible at first to comprehend how Palestine can be so small. Accustomed as we are to have our history spread over so much ground, it is at first incomprehensible. But soon it appears that this was not a great people, and that their country was filled full to the uttermost. The doings of the kings of Samaria and the wars with the kings of Judah were petty struggles, while all the time we have exalted them into national combats. Through these plains below us there was once raging a mighty people, driving from their homes the enfeebled Canaanites. So, too, the Assyrian, sweeping over the region round about, passed this and left it desolate when the Israelites had in their turn become enfeebled. From this point so much of Old Testament story comes to mind that one scarcely realizes what a vantage ground it is. The mind refuses to comprehend all that would suggest itself, and the listless air of the dragoman, who is, no doubt, heartily tired of it all, brings us back to real life once more.

But one historical scene must be mentioned be-

fore we go. Here Joshua assembled the tribes after
the capture of Ai. The curse was to be put on
Ebal, the blessing on Gerizim. Between the two
stood the Levites with the ark. It is a curious fact
that the acoustic properties of this valley render it
quite possible to carry on a conversation with people
on the mountains, although the tops of the mountains are two miles apart. A line of telegraph poles
running through the valley east to Gilead strikes
one as singular. To have civilization brought into
this region seems out of place.

We at last turn our backs on the ruins and seek
our horses, which have been left with an attendant
on the west side of
the mountain. After
a little distance we
strike into the di-
rect road leading to
Nablous, which we
can distinguish be-

low among olive trees and orchards. The road
is terribly steep for the first part of the distance, but
grows better as we proceed. We come among trees
and ride over a bridge, and then we find ourselves
beside a brook which flows along in great volume.
Around are gardens, and the city below is really
beautiful as seen at this distance.

Nablous, or Neapolis as it should be, is the old
city of Shechem, and its white houses and pictur-

esque towers stand in the valley which completely shuts it in, nestling there like some child in the lap of its mother. The outside is very attractive, but the inside is disappointing. The young Englishman, whom I shall call Hilton, although what his name really was I have no idea, and myself, ambitious, as usual, rode on ahead of our party and trusted to our own instincts to find the camp. We knew it was to be near the city somewhere, but we were entirely ignorant in which direction. So for a time it began to look gloomy, but we pressed on, secure of finding something if we only persevered, and at last, under some olive trees to the west of the town, we found the tents already up. Hilton and myself dismounted and proceeded to view the outside of the place, for we had not enough courage to venture in alone. Not that we had no desire, for the city, as we rode into camp, lying a little below us, was so attractive that our first impulse was to explore it. The dragoman was late in coming into camp, for he had to look after the tender ones of his flock, each and every woman demanding his especial care. Around us were ragged children and a few grown people, who stared in curiosity to see what kind of effects we would have. The tents were open and unprotected, our baggage easily transportable, but nothing was missing, although I was somewhat anxious. Shortly after the main part of our number came up we had a visit from a mis-

sionary in the town, who came to offer us any courtesies which might lie in his way. I felt he was
very good, but I distrusted his appearance. He was
large, sleek, and apparently well fed. The Philologist of the party was a member of some board of
Foreign Missions, and thus was greatly interested in
everything pertaining to the missionaries. At once
he began to ask questions, which this man answered

with a fluency which delighted him.
We were then induced to visit his
school. Thus we wandered through
the heart of the town, which was, I
think, the vilest place I ever pene-
trated. Jerusalem, so famed for its
nastiness, is a paradise compared to it.
What makes the contrast more striking
is the fact that Nablous is the center
of great soap industries. The people
here advertise well. They keep the
city outwardly very clean, or it keeps
itself clean, but within they certainly do not make
use of their advantages. The pathway led through
a mass of refuse, and was so narrow that great care
was needful to keep from contamination.

We found the school of the missionary, visited his
house, which seemed gloomy, and then went to see
the Samaritan Codex which is kept here. The
synagogue is a small oblong chamber, and the rolls
are kept in a recess at one side, and, as they are

covered with silk, one sees but little of that which is inside. The oldest of all is not shown. The others are, of course, only copies, and comparatively modern. The most ancient is not older, probably, than the seventh century.

There is not much to see in Nablous ; indeed, one walk through the town is amply sufficient. I have so little fancy for the Samaritans, who were, it strikes me, quite as bigoted as the Jews, that I think, as there are not more than two hundred, they deserve very little attention. One thing I noticed as curious. The Protestants will not send any one to teach these people unless they be allowed to teach all the Old and the New Testament. I should think if one wished to teach Christianity it were well to begin with the Pentateuch.

The young Englishman whom I call Hilton was singular in several ways. In the first place he seemed very much averse from telling his name. Naturally, as he would not set us straight, we were the more anxious to know just what it was. So it happened that he was known by a different name by every member of the party. I hope he enjoyed it, but it was exceedingly annoying to me to feel uncertain every time I addressed him, whether I got it right or not. Then, too, with pure English exclusiveness, he seemed to have a kind of contempt for each one of us, which, while he did not exhibit it to me, amused me because I was quite certain that I came in for my share. Owing to his little peculiarities I did not offer him that deference which I should otherwise have shown, and from this reason I am firmly convinced he became attached to me. In our tent, which he shared with myself and another American, we had occasional disputes. While the furniture was all equally divided, and my tin wash-basin was entirely my own, there was a great scarcity of chairs. One little stool was supposed to do for the three. Consequently the one who first retired piled his effects on the stool. The next one who came piled his on top. Then the third, essaying to do the same, rolled them all on the ground. This difficulty once settled, Hilton and myself had another grievance. Our companion snored. Politeness forbade us for some time to throw things at his head, and we used to lie awake and converse on the subject. Finally we decided it would be only the part of charity to inform him that he snored, and give him a chance to reform. We did so. The result was most unexpected. He denied it, in fact said he had never snored in his life. We were staggered. There was nothing to do but to wait. To contradict him was to bring on more vehement assertion.

In the middle of the night we were awakened by the noise, and, having exhausted our patience, we resolved to wake him and try to prove to him what were our feelings. It made no difference. He was only furious at being aroused, and we were left to console each other as best we could. So long hours were consumed by us in talk, which possibly drew us together into something like friendship. Hilton was a good fellow, but had a purely English way of showing it. While he was a gentleman in every respect, he so often curbed a desire to be rude that I was excessively amused. He lacked that polish which rendered the Hungarians attractive, although he was, I fancy, far more intelligent than they. He was about the only Englishman whom I have met who seemed able to comprehend an American joke. Altogether he was very agreeable, and without him I should have missed a great deal of pleasure in going through the country.

In the evening we gathered around the table in the dining-tent, and, with a smoking candle to give us light, attempted to read. But it was a useless attempt. Some played cards, and while this was in itself perfectly harmless, it seemed, somehow, out of place. In traveling in these sacred spots one ought, seemingly, to be given entirely to devotional literature and religious exercises. The reverse is apt to be the case. Seated this evening at the table were the Presbyterian from Pennsylvania and the young man from London. The latter was a ritualist of the most pronounced type. Strange to say, he fraternized with the Presbyterian, and occasionally got any amount of snubbing. In search of relief he would come to me to have the priestly sanction for his statements, and then return and crush the Presbyterian, which, of course, led to interminable arguments upon church polity. Hilton and myself were, perhaps, not half reverent enough when these two began their disputes. It lay quite naturally in my power to say the wrong thing at the right time, and so the fire would be set burning, which I would either precipitate upon my own head or, perhaps, by some good fortune quench when it became a little wearisome. Mr. C——, the young man in question, was as harmless and as innocent as it was possible for an Englishman to be. He was evidently trained in all the beliefs of the advanced school, but found them extremely impracticable on this journey. A woman was in the party whose religious tendencies were of the same high order. The young man she appropriated to herself, and as she was not old and a widow, I felt then, and still feel, that she had no objection to changing her state. This, however, the young man did not perceive. So with these contending elements we started upon our journey, hardly with a prospect of bettering our condition, but still with the hope that we might reach Beirût without serious clashing.

XIII.

In Samaria.

In leaving Nablous we departed without the admiration with which we approached it. Our way lay toward Samaria, at no great distance to the northwest. The road runs down the valley, which is very beautiful, but soon it turns up a gentle hill, and passing by a village we found we were hardly on the right track, for we had been following Mr. C——'s dragoman, who knew, apparently, as little of the road as I myself. Villages are upon every height, the landscape is still rich and flourishing, and after we have climbed a bald ridge we find the city of Samaria before us, perched upon a broad, isolated hill. The valleys all around are pleasant and smooth, and the town itself occupies a place of great natural strength. Although not high, still the sides seem abrupt, and are now laid out in terraces, formed doubtless of the stones by which the ancient city was built. It was founded by Omri, King of Israel, and was the capital of the Ten Tribes until the Captivity. Before this there had been no fixed capital, but as the new kingdom was the result of a rebellion, it was ruled by a succession of adventurers, who dwelt wherever their fancy dictated. Shechem was first chosen by Jeroboam, then the beauty of Tirzah seduced his affections. His successor endeavored to build Ramah, but misfortune drove him back to Tirzah. After the death of Baasha, who was defeated in building Ramah, his son reigned only two years, when Zimri, captain of half his chariots, conspired against him. So, as he was drunk in the house of his steward, Zimri killed him and all his following, and reigned in his stead. One cannot but be struck with the naïve way in which the Sacred Writ records all these barbarities. But Zimri, it appears, reigned only seven days in Tirzah, truly a reign of blood. Then the people made Omri, captain of the host, king, and went up and besieged Tirzah. Zimri, who was an encouraging bandit, went into the king's house and burnt it down over his head and perished. Thus it happened that there were two parties, one following Omri and the other Tibni. Omri at last prevailed and reigned all alone. It must have been almost as uncomfortable to be a ruler in those days as it is now. It does not appear that Omri was any better than his predecessors, for when they both died the Sacred Writ records that they perished because of their sins. This man Omri bought the hill of Samaria for two talents of silver, doubtless with a keen eye to real estate, and built thereon the city, which he named after the owner of the hill. So the sins of Omri, who died about this time, did not kill him off until he had enjoyed the regal honor for eleven years. He left his interesting son Ahab to reign in his stead. The history of this king, and his crafty wife Jezebel, is familiar to every child.

Three separate kings of Syria, named Ben Hadad, besieged Samaria, one during the reign of Omri, and two in the time of Ahab. The first attack during the reign of Ahab was repulsed by a small band of Israelites, who found the Syrian king and his followers drunk. It may seem strange that seven thousand men could overcome thirty-two kings with their followers. Either kingly dignity was at a low ebb, almost as it is at present in Germany, or the royal revelers were greatly overcome by the subtle tempter. The next siege of interest was when the four leprous men who sat at the gate, seeing no use to wait longer, went into the tents of Syrians, to find everything deserted, silver and gold and raiment. Truly this was a scene worthy of the Arabian Nights, and in childhood I loved to linger over this story, picturing vividly the city where the famine was so great that people to live could consent to boil their children ; and the camp was filled with riches.

So with one thought and another in mind, first that of seeing all this valley filled with Syrians, and then of Ahab, who was something of a king, less parvenu than his fellows; then his royal wife, who introduced so much wickedness and idolatry into a country which had enough of that; afterward the severe figure of Elijah, whose presence, I fancy, was a great annoyance to these luxury-loving people; then the milder Elisha, who was in every way a worthy successor to the great prophet, if not so austere, —all these make this place and this period a most interesting study.

The difficulty must always be to connect that harmless mound, which, although large, is hardly more than a hill, with such stirring events. To-day it looks so peaceful as it stands in so fertile a valley surrounded by hills, which, for the first time since we left Jerusalem, appear to be cultivated to their very tops. Indeed, this landscape is the only one which has appeared entirely agreeable, in which, in fact, there has not been some suggestion of desolation. Others may have been beautiful, but none have seemed so rich and prosperous. Around on the hills are signs of habitation, which, of themselves, add to the effect. Groves appear at different points, and the trees at the foot of the hill of Sama-

14

ria nearly fill the valley. On the hill itself there seem to be many trees of different kinds, although, presumably, the great majority are olive.

The present population of Sebastieh is not over four hundred souls. It stands midway on the eastern side, and is built of the ruins of the former city. The ruined church of St. John is the first object to be seen, perched on the top of the hill where the village is placed. Going down through the valley we ride across it to the foot of the hill, and by a road which leads up to the church we soon come among the huts of the natives. They look more

comfortable than in other places, sitting down wherever it pleases their fancy. The church was built by the Knights of St. John in honor of their patron saint the Baptist, who was, according to tradition, buried here. The ruins are not interesting, except as a remnant of that prodigious energy which western nations showed in establishing throughout all this country churches and castles of great magnificence.

Going up the hill we come to some columns, remnants of the splendor with which Herod sought to make this city beautiful. Fifteen in one place show where he erected a temple, probably in honor of Augustus. Around the city at other points stand long colonnades, which were, doubtless, the columns erected by him to ornament the main street of the city. To-day their white shafts stand as a memorial of the evanescent ambition of a turbulent man. The course of Herod is not unlike adventurers of the present day. Every once in a while the world sees the rise of some meteor, which flashes up for a short time and then dies out, leaving nothing but ruins behind it.

Thus we lingered around the place, the center of Israelitish history as Jerusalem was of Jewish history, almost unwilling to set out for regions which might prove less attractive. Owing to the slowness of some of the party, for there are always a few who insist upon seeing everything, even though it be only a mound of dirt, we who were more ambitious took Mr. C——'s dragoman and set out, intending to meet at some given point agreed upon between the two dragomans. We went down the hill into the plain, crossed that and climbed the hill to the other side. When we had reached the top it occurred to our dragoman to wonder whether he had come the right road. This placed us in a very uncomfortable position. We could see nothing of the rest of the party behind, and if we returned they would have gone down the other way out of sight, so that altogether it began to look hopeless. But we cheered up the poor fellow, who, being an Arab, lacked confidence, and we plunged on. The country was pleasant, and we did not greatly fear getting lost, for we could inquire our way to Jenin, if it were necessary, although in that case we should have to go without our luncheon. Had we taken the precaution to have Luigi with us we should then have been entirely independent. At last our dragoman became so uncertain that a council of war was formed, and we decided that it was best to strike the main road and wait until the rest of the party came up. After a little trouble, in which we were obliged to climb the steep side of an intervening hill, we came to a pleasant spot where the road which the other party must take lay full in view. As the sun was now getting pretty high in the heavens, indeed had already begun its downward course, we thought more of Luigi than we ought, perhaps.

I notice that writers on the Holy Land leave out the most interesting details, namely, their own personal experiences. To read most of that which is written one would suppose that the travelers were consumed entirely by thought upon religious subjects, and ignored with positive heroism the more prosaic but at the same time more interesting part of the journey. While the history of the country serves as an admirable background, the little annoyances and pleasures of the journey must be the most interesting part to every one except the dry pedant. Thus, when we sat around on the hillside, with our horses tethered near by, scanning the distant road for some sign of human beings, we were as little solicitous about the ancient history of the place as though we had been perched upon a Berkshire hill. The widow was the only lady in our detachment, and she soon consoled herself by the conversation of Mr. C——, who was the reverse of fluent. The young man had been a " clark " in a London store, I fancy ground down to poverty on meager pay, so that nothing in him was allowed to grow unless it was his ritualistic proclivities, which somehow flourish under the most adverse circumstances. A relation, after the way English relations have—I wish American aunts would follow the example—left him a fortune. His first idea was to see the Holy Land. He had never seen anything before but London. This was his first plunge into the great world, and when I thought of his pounds, shillings and pence, and also of his innocence, I trembled. While in Jerusalem he decided that he would not be safe without a private dragoman. Somehow he had been left out in one of our excursions around the Holy City, and this so piqued him, and at the same time so frightened him,

that Cook humanely, and of course for a considera-
tion, gave him the dragoman who was at present
threatening the digestions of all our contingent, by
taking us so far from Luigi. The clergy of the
party took it more patiently than the rest, which
may seem strange when their appetites are considered, and looked upon the digression as a lark.
Indeed, it was an experience, and the fact is, that
traveling in this country is becoming rather too tame
for complete enjoyment.

The dragoman looked sulky and anxious, but we
bore up bravely, with the exception of the widow,
who, being thoroughly English, could ill afford to
have her stomach neglected. Even Mr. C—— could
not satisfy this ambition, and so as the hours rolled
on we became more and more anxious to see Luigi.
At last he came. The others had lunched already,
and we seized the remnants with an avidity which
proved conclusively that we were traveling for
pleasure and not for instruction.

When Leighton came up we hastily drew ourselves
together, the dragoman got a fine scolding in Arabic,
which Leighton used with such a fluency that I would
recommend it to all fiery people as a medium of
expressing their feelings. The afternoon was far
spent, for we had lingered long in waiting for the
others, while they also had waited for us at the
place where they lunched. Leighton hastened matters a little, urging on the English lady, Mrs. W——,

who was afraid to ride fast, until we soon passed into a rocky dell with precipices on either side. Some one saw a gazelle, but I failed to get a sight of it. The dragoman regretted he could not shoot it, and so did we, for mutton and chicken, the only meat we could get, were becoming a trifle tiresome. So shortly, just as the light was growing dim, we rode out into the beautiful plain of Dothan. Dothan, where the sons of Jacob fed their flocks, and a youth came to learn if they were well! The plain was rich and green, apparently over-spreading the hills on either side with its lovely verdure. The road was here almost entirely without stones, lying in the middle between the hills.

Through this we galloped, for we were not yet in sight of our camp and we must hasten. So, willy nilly, the timid lady must press on. But here, as we passed in rapid fashion, we recollected that Elisha lived when the Syrians came to invade the land. He gave notice to the king, and Ben Hadad tried to capture him, and thus deprive the Israelites of their informant. Elisha's servant coming to him, cried in terror that the plain was filled with horsemen and chariots, and then his master opened his eyes and he saw the hosts of the Lord around to protect him. The Syrians were smitten with blindness, and led away to Samaria. Passing down a rocky road we came to some olive trees, and then ascending we found at last the tents which were waiting for us.

So dark was it that we could not see our surroundings, nor observe that Jenin was near at hand. But we were well content to rest, for we had had several experiences which caused our familiar camp to seem like home.

XIV.

Esdraelon.

JENIN is a very considerable place, having about three thousand inhabitants. But it did not appear to be so large from our camp, for directly in front of us was a thick cactus hedge, and to the right was a large olive orchard. As we had had no time the night before to look around, we took the opportunity to do so in the morning. Off to the north spread out the great plain of Esdraelon, with its low elevations and beautiful country. Jenin was hid behind trees, and was all the more interesting for that, I fancy. Three palms stood up in solitary grandeur directly in front of us, while around was our camp equipage. The dragoman had promised an easy day, and we were delighted with the pros-

pect, for we had climbed hills and wrestled with
steep places enough to require a rest. So when we
at last got ready, we started off in merry fashion,
riding through a part of the town, which was as deserted and as desolate at that time of day as could
well be imagined. At the other side of the town
we saw a mosque with a tall minaret and a solitary
palm standing by it. The whole was a perfect picture, and I should have been remiss, indeed, had I
failed to transcribe it to my note-book. A high
hedge of cactus stood around it and a camel in front
of it. But the camel I omitted. I had but little
time, and hastened for fear I should get lost. While
it is, perhaps, not so bad to get lost when some one
in the party speaks Arabic, to be entirely without
any means of communication would be extremely
disagreeable.

To the right rise the rocky mountains of Gilboa,
infested in times past by Bedouins, who now obey
Turkish rule, and, out of deference to their guns,
behave themselves. From here to the foot of the
hills before Nazareth is just fourteen miles in a
straight line. But our way lies in among some of the
hills on the eastern border of the plain and we shall
have much farther to go before we reach them. As
we ascend a little rise of ground we see the whole
length of the plain of Esdraelon stretched out before us.

The ancient plain of Megiddo was, and may yet

be, the battle-ground of Palestine. Beautiful beyond question, it is the center of the wealth of this coun-

try, for from this point in every direction the rocks begin to appear. Here they are covered by earth, and everywhere there is evidence of cultivation and fertility. Every acre of this plain is now under cultivation. The richness of the soil is almost beyond belief. The Sultan owns half and the Sursock family of Beirût own the rest. Were the government only stable who would not wish to settle in such a paradise? With the  climate all that could possibly be desired, with ground capable of anything, with this glorious vision before one, surely here might be made a true home. So as the eye gazes up this enormous stretch of country, which is so placed that from our standpoint almost every part is brought into view, one cannot but reflect upon the history which has been made on this spot. Yonder lies Carmel, standing out from the rest of the landscape in glorious prominence, with its sides sloping off smoothly into the plain. To the north rise the lower hills of Galilee, and to the right beyond a height lies the chasm of the Jordan. The eye never grows weary, never

tires of this fair scene. But gazing off over the
green carpet which spreads out before, one reflects
that throughout this country Ahab and Elijah, perhaps two as interesting characters as we have in the
Books of the Kings, were wont to come, and held
that unequal contest always going on, the power of
truth against the armies of sin and the world. On
Carmel yonder Elijah performed that memorable
sacrifice so prominent in the mind of every educated
person.

Just back of us is the place where Saul and his

noble-hearted son, Jonathan, fell. So after a ride
of several miles we climb a low hill with a village
perched upon its top, and find ourselves in Jezreel.
There are not more than twenty houses now in the
hamlet, but around are ruins, and more than three
hundred subterranean granaries for storing corn.
Standing on this point the plain appears to its best
advantage. Here is where Ahab, royal man if he
was wicked, built his palace.   Here three successive

monarchs reigned, and I must confess I admire the taste of these kings of Israel who selected places so fitting for royalty to dwell in.

Below us was the vineyard which the greed of a king demanded, and thus poor Naboth became the unlucky object of Jezebel's craft. Then when the stern Elijah, who must have been a perfect torture to poor Ahab, so much led around by his wife, appeared, and Ahab said, " Hast thou found me out, mine enemy ? " He answered, " I have found thee." Surely Elijah must have been worse than a conscience. The terrible denunciation of the prophet must have caused many anxious hours to the king, although I greatly doubt if Jezebel much cared for what he said. Well might the Scriptures say: " But there was none like Ahab, who did sell himself to work wickedness in the sight of the Lord, whom Jezebel, his wife, stirred up." Surely a wicked woman can cause her husband a great deal of misery.

From Jezreel the watchman saw Jehu driving furiously, and sent word to the kings of Judah and Israel. On this blood-stained site Jezebel was slain and devoured by the dogs in the street. A little more than a mile from here was the ancient Shunem where lived the Shunammite woman and her son. Here Elisha, humane, sweet-tempered prophet, lived in his little chamber over the wall. Doubtless, here came the great Naaman from Damacus to be healed, and thence went in great wrath because Elisha was too patriotic, as it seemed to him.

Then, on this plain which lies out before us, Barak rushed down upon the hosts of Sisera, who, having chariots, could not fight to advantage, because the ground was heavy with rain. Here Josiah came to fight with Necho, the king of Egypt, and received his death-wound. So, from generation to generation, Esdraelon has been a scene of plunder. Its fertility has attracted the different kings, and its level ground has become a marching place for armies. It might almost be called the center of Israelite history, so many have been the famous battles fought here. A little farther on we come to Fûleh, which was more recently the scene of a battle between the Turks and the French under Kleber. With a handful of men, fifteen hundred at best, he kept the enemy at bay for six hours, although they consisted of twenty-five thousand soldiers. As he was becoming worsted, Napoleon, with only six hundred, came to his relief, and the Turks, thinking a large army was upon them, fled.

From here we turn to the right, passing around to the northern slope of Gilboa, and come to the fountain where Gideon drank with his men. The water issues from under a rock and forms a large pool. Here the three hundred lapped the water as a dog lappeth, and the Lord said, " By the three hundred which lapped I will save you." The val-

ley was filled with Midianites and Amalekites, and
Gideon, dividing his band into three parties, put a
trumpet in every man's hand and also gave them
empty pitchers with lights in the pitchers. By and
by a cry rang through the air: "The sword of the
Lord and of Gideon." Then every
man brake his pitcher and the light
streamed forth. A panic seized the
host, and they fled in their confusion, mistaking their neighbors for
enemies. In the same place Saul
pitched his camp. Samuel, on whose
advice he relied, was dead, and he
resorted to the witch who lived yonder at Endor.

As we come over to Nain, a miserable village on the northern slope
of Little Hermon, we see Tabor
before us. But we cannot forget
that here our Lord, touched with
infinite pity at seeing the funeral procession of an
only son, stopped and raised him from the dead.
To be sure the filth of the place is such to-day that
it seems hard to connect our Lord with it, but,
undoubtedly, this is the true spot. In that day,
probably, it was a better place, a larger town, no
doubt, and not a mass of mud hovels scarcely raised
above the ground.

Indeed, it seems strange how it is possible for

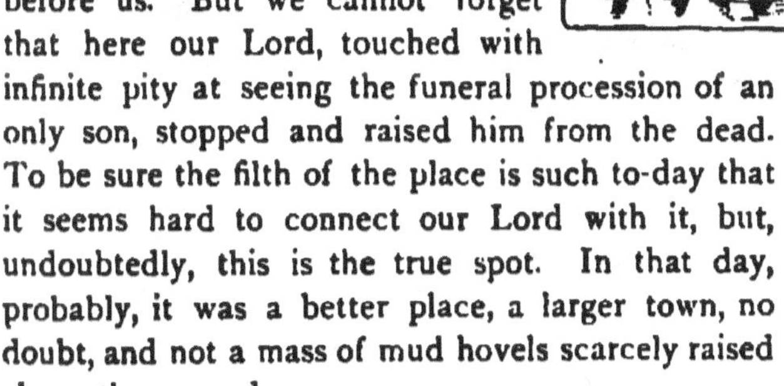

these people to live as they do.   Here on the edge
of a great and fertile tract of country they exist like

so many brutes.   From the position on
the north-eastern side of Little Hermon
the view is even finer than from Jezreel.
For here the valley of the branch of the
river Kishon runs off toward the Jordan.   From Mount Carmel to the chasm
of the Jordan there is an uninterrupted
view.   Across this arm of the valley
rise the hills which hide Nazareth.   Between lies a beautiful country, fair to
look upon ; behind us the mountain.

From here one sees clearly the possibility of a
railway, such as has been for some time projected.
So great is the produce of this region, that to convey one year's crop to the port of Haifa costs fifty

thousand dollars. As a large part of the country is owned by the Sultan, it is hoped soon to accomplish this object. It is proposed to build it to connect the sea with the Hauran, that great tract of country lying to the east of the Jordan. If it once opens up this region, it is extremely probable that it will be extended to Damascus, since, when once built across the Jordan, the cost of extension would not be very great. It is a great pity that the slowness and the wavering policy of the Government should stand in the way. Once the plans were almost completed, but owing to delay they lapsed. It is not improbable that the next few years will see the railroad in operation, for no great difficulty could be in the way, since, from the sea to the Jordan, there is very little mountain to hinder the builders.

But perhaps the most fascinating, although by no means the most practicable project, is that of the Duke of Sutherland, who proposes to cut a canal through the plain lying below us, and flood the whole of the Jordan chasm or "ghor." Already surveys have been made and estimates given. The great difference between them is a little amusing. Owing to the great questions which would arise, as well as from the opposition of those interested in the Suez Canal, a great deal of feeling has been excited. One party shows conclusively that the cost could not exceed £8,000,000, while the other demonstrates that it would amount to £225,573,648 and a few odd shillings. I think it quite as well to discard the few shillings. Already £10,000 have been subscribed for surveys. The Sultan at first opposed, but now approves. Fifteen hundred square miles would be submerged, a tract extending from near Banias on the north to a distance far below the Dead Sea, and reaching from one range of mountains to the other standing on either side of the river Jordan.

The difficulties which lie in the way are the great political interests which are involved. Great Britain would gain such an influence in this quarter as virtually to annex Palestine to England, which, I think, would be a good thing. Then the other governments of Europe would rebel at this disturbance of the balance of power. A cut made from the sea at Haifa would flood the valley in five years if it were two hundred feet wide and forty feet deep. Then, in order to make it of practical advantage, another cut would have to be made from the Dead Sea to the Red Sea. This, it is thought, would be a feat almost without parallel. When the Panama Canal is once opened, then this scheme will appear more feasible. Besides all this, a vast amount of fertile land would be rendered useless, which would, it is true, be offset by the opening up of vast tracts now comparatively waste on the east of the Jordan.

It has occurred to me that if Palestine is to be

again inhabited by the children of Israel, there is no way better than this to accomplish the purpose. For when placed between two large sheets of water, it must, of necessity, become moist and liable to a copious rain-fall. Thus the hills, with little encouragement, would bring forth some kind of vegetation, and trees could be made to grow. When the hills are once covered with foliage, the valleys will soon assume their former richness. A little co-operation

on the part of Hebrew colonists—and there seems to be a tendency just at present to that end—would bring the whole country, in a marvelously short period of time, to a state which most people do not realize. It seems almost a pity that some great Jewish banker who has an enormous amount of money at his disposal does not attempt something of the kind. Even if the canal is not cut through to the Red Sea, the inland lake joined with the sea at Haifa would be such a splendid means of communication with the interior that it would shortly pay for the expense. It is certainly the only way the country can be saved, for thus it could be wrested from the hands of the Turk, and at the same time be brought back to fertility.

But then they say sentimental people would cry out at having the beautiful Sea of Galilee submerged and all the historic sites on its banks buried six hundred feet under water. I would propose that the " ghor " be flooded and left so until Palestine became fairly well cultivated, and then to close the canal and let the lake dry up, as it will do when left to itself. Thus two objects could be accomplished, the sentimentalists would be satisfied, and the country restored. Something, doubtless, will be done in the near future which will give this country greater prominence than it has had before. The subject is one which the different nations cannot ignore much longer. With a little less selfishness on the part of rulers the country most favored, I do believe, on the face of the earth by climate, would become of some use to mankind. At present the country is as safe as almost any other. This seems the more remarkable, since, from the place where I am standing, there is scarcely a dwelling to be seen. All is open country, and the few inhabitants live in villages clustered together in some quiet nook.

So passing down from the elevation we ride across this beautiful land, crossing the stream, which is not large, and pass on until we come to the foot of the hills and begin to take our way to Nazareth. We are under the leadership of Mr. C——'s dragoman who takes us, very willing, up the almost sheer precipice of the hill. As we rise from the plain the view extends out in every direction, and Carmel looks especially grand as it shuts out the view to the sea. Soon, however, we plunge into a rocky ravine, which appears to be almost on the top of the hill, and then wandering around, as it seems, in a hopeless fashion over roads if possible worse than any we have yet had, we come to the top of a hill where we catch the first glimpse of Nazareth, the home of our Lord, lying there among the hills, nestling in this quiet nook peaceful and serene ; yes, even beautiful after our rough ride, which has hardly led us to expect such pleasant things. So down into the valley we go, and soon reach a decent road once more, and see the tents pitched on the opposite side of the town. To reach them we pass around, and not through, the village, and dismount from our horses with great satisfaction, for we are to spend Sunday here and rest. I for one was pleased, for to ride one whole week over such roads as we had had was trying to the best of tempers.

XV.

Nazareth.

ONE always comes home with a certain sense of satisfaction, because I fancy it is the most restful of places. So I would argue that the more tired a man feels the more he appreciates the home-feeling. To be traveling around in nomadic fashion without any established resting-place would hardly appear to give a homelike impression. But truly the door of my tent welcomed me like an old friend, and although it was twenty miles perhaps from its last resting-place, yet when once I was within its walls all was the same. It was home for the time being. The same group of tents around made the feeling stronger, the same familiar countenances were like faithful domestics, even the animals of this traveling menagerie had a sort of welcome when we came in

from our day's journey.   It rarely happened that we
saw them on the march, because they took other
paths, which led them by a direct route to their
destination.   This night we found everything in
readiness, even my luggage was placed in the same
position as I left it, and within the tent it was hard
to realize that we had progressed at all.   Then
when I wished for something, there was Luigi who
came to my call, or that other waiter, the Arab,
whose black eyes haunt me yet.   These were my
first impressions of Nazareth.   How strange ! I
hear the sentimental reader say.   I fancy if you, my
dear friend, will try horseback all day you may then
appreciate the satisfaction one has of getting off and
sitting down to rest.

Nazareth is just outside, but I am too tired to
appreciate the fact ; so while I am lying on my bed
seeking, shall I confess it, a little sleep, and, may I
add, not getting it, there come crowding into my
mind a few thoughts of the place.   We are to spend
the Sabbath here.   How well it was ordered !
Surely Cook, if he has no heart, has, at least, some
soul.   But then I must forget Cook; if I do not the
whole stay here will be spoiled.

Nazareth !   Ah ! yes, it is coming to me now.
The place next to Jerusalem which is dearest to the
Christian's heart !   Perhaps dearer, because in this
place was spent that angelic period of our Lord's
life, the youth, which to every man is his best and

purest experience. So it was with Him, a period
so sinless, so peaceful, so sweet, as we contemplate
His humble life led in this place. Nazareth does
not cry out for vengeance. Nazareth, to be sure,
rejected Him, but it did not torture Him until we
feel almost as though we hated the place. No, the
people here now are mostly those who have gathered
out of love for His sacred name, those who revere
the Divinity in the man. So, perhaps, this is the
most peaceful spot in all Palestine, for here we have
no thought of His anguish, only of His disappointment, because in His own country the greatest
Prophet found no honor.

And then is not this the place where the sweet
Mother lived who gave to men the truest example
of mother-love? Here first, they say, the Annunciation was made. Here in this spot was the first evidence of God revealed in human form. Surely we
have no time to sleep, I must arise and look without.
There are the tents, the horses, the asses, the luggage scattered around, while Leighton is going from
one tent to another, busy about something, I care
not what. There sit the people of the party. They
are talking. Yes, even the two Presbyterian clergymen are laughing, while Mr. C—— is off somewhere
with the widow. I am greatly of the opinion that
these people are waiting for their dinner, for I find
that the young Englishman, whose name is something like Hilton, and the obstinate American are

watching the old Arab who caters so acceptably to the inner man. This is the present; I was thinking of the past. It is useless for me to linger longer; I begin to feel a fellow sympathy with my friends. Yet, methinks, that here one ought not to eat.

I find there is no use to remain within the tent, and with a weary air and with a sketch-book in

hand I seek the general company. As I have said, all around are the party, and near the outskirts is my horse. Poor animal! By this time I was well accustomed to his skinny and dilapidated appearance. Indeed, I had forgotten all about the dreadful sore he had on his side. So I sat down to sketch him, since I wanted a better subject, with a kind of pity, as though I ought to have something in the future by which to remember him. He was not very picturesque, and the thick padding they kept on his back all the time did not add to his appearance. Then my thoughts turned to the donkey who stood with such inimitable patience just by his side. There is such unutterable repose in a donkey's face. I wonder why some of our sentimental artists have not sought for some effects from his quiet countenance.

The sun was going down rapidly, and the air was becoming chill before the dinner was ready, but the whole party remained outside the tents with commendable courage, waiting for the welcome sound of the horn. Of course the meal was pleasant, nay, almost jovial. We had every reason to be happy. Indeed, the party as a whole was perhaps especially well constituted for enjoying itself. The members were withal suited to each other ; not perhaps too similar, but sufficiently unlike to be amusing, each to the other, while not so different as to be disagreeable.

After dinner we were treated to the company of Leighton, who was not averse from sitting down with us in friendly chat and drinking whisky, which some one of the party provided. Leighton was a clever fellow. He urged upon us so strongly the necessity of taking large supplies of a stuff we did not want and never drank, that we each laid in something like two quarts of the insidious fluid, which for some reason disappeared utterly when we reached Beirût. For this I did not much care. It was an incumbrance to me, I took it because I was frightened into the belief that if I got wet I should surely die on the road, unless I had a little liquor to warm me up. I found out afterward that Leighton was much addicted to drink.   Then I was sorry that I had, for my part, put temptation in his way.   He said, to be sure, that the Arabs had stolen the wine and the liquor, but I am fully convinced that the entire amount reported missing went down his thirsty throat.   Poor Leighton, cast on a foreign shore, surrounded by tee-totalers—for they tell me that Mohammed anticipated the W. C. T. U.—either inherited or acquired an appetite, which I fancy is to-day leaving him stranded in Jaffa, waiting, alas ! for an appointment to guide a party through the country.   I was told that Mr. Cook or his agent, philanthropic men, moved with magnanimous pity, took poor Leighton this trip on trial.   They were so sorry for him, but for us, poor wanderers on a foreign and barbarous soil, they had no mercy.   I should like to have Mr. Cook go through Thibet with a dragoman who was addicted to drink.   Fortunately we had Mr. C——'s dragoman who could have translated the Arabic for us in case we came utterly to grief : but more of Leighton anon.

This evening I had a little argument with the Philologist.   In fact, we were always having some kind of a dispute.   Probably that is why we took so kindly to each other.   When it was not the peculiarities of the English language it was about American ignorance, a subject on which we agreed perfectly for a time.   At last he could not hide the English which was in him, and remarked that there were no Americans who were so cultivated as his countrymen. I could not endure this, so I rebelled.

"But," he said, "take this party. Now there are three American clergymen. Take yourself, for instance ; what do you know about philology ?"

"Nothing whatever," I said. "But what do you know about theology ?" He saw the point. He did not dare to answer, for he was an intelligent man.

"But," said he, turning the subject, "you are not a studious people."

"But we are," I insisted.

"Take these three clergymen," he replied. "They are all reading French novels."

"True," I remarked, "but you loaned them. Not one of us brought a work of fiction with us."

This was a fact. He had given us some very good books, worth reading, but undeniably fiction. One ought not to read novels in the Holy Land. But then we did it.

"Well," said I, after a little pause, "you see how you have led us astray. We don't study philology. We are meditating ; taking a vacation, in fact." The old gentleman turned his nose up in air, a little doubtful, perhaps, about our acquirements, but I kept a bold front. I was not going to admit to him that the average American clergyman was a dunce.

At other times we used to argue about pronunciation.   I fancy it is possible for the two nations to dispute upon this subject forever.   As a rule, however, we agreed pretty well.   He was complimentary enough to say that educated Americans spoke as well as educated Englishmen.   Occasionally I used to tease him a little about the H.   He did not mind it ; at least, so I thought.   But one night at dinner I was talking, when he spoke up sharply and said :

"You dropped an H then."   I was angry, of course.   In fact, who would not be ?   My first impulse was to show it, but then I thought better of it and said :

"Yes, I think I did.   We Americans esteem it polite at times."   But he was a very nice man, and so broad for an Englishman that I actually came to the point of paying him a great compliment.   I said he was just like an American.   I must confess I think he was a little surprised, but I simply obeyed a good impulse, and what could he have expected more ?

The next morning we went to church, which was certainly a privilege in this country.   The English Mission has two morning services, one in Arabic and the other in English.   As I declined to preach, the Presbyterian from Pennsylvania consented.   Surely Episcopalians are liberal enough.   Previously this man had been so unkind as to throw our little failing, namely, not inviting other ministers into our pulpits, into my face.   As I was innocent I felt a little aggrieved. I had never refused to invite a Presbyterian minister into my pulpit; why, pray, should I be abused for the sins of my brethren? But now he had been invited, and my first impulse on leaving the church was to ask him if he did not feel better about us. He had no reply to make. Poor man! I could not understand him. He had shortly before complained at not being invited to preach in one of our churches, and as soon as he had the opportunity he did not seem to appreciate it. I really fancy he thought a mission station, being so far from a bishop, did not count.

Evidently he wished to create some kind of sensation. Poor dear man, he little thought how very few Episcopal clergy would in the least mind having him in their pulpits. It is all the bishops, those terrible bishops, who keep us within bounds. I would therefore take this opportunity to suggest to discontented ministers who have a desire to preach in our pulpits to carry their complaints to head-quarters. I for one am just a little weary of being abused for episcopal sins, if one may term them such.

The English Church is a handsome stone structure in the Gothic style, well equipped for the work, which is, I fancy, extremely small. At least at the

English service our party was fully half the congregation, even without the widow and Mr. C——, who had slipped off and gone to the Greek church as being "more of a service." Besides, I believe their church-feelings were shocked to have a Presbyterian preach in a consecrated chapel. I hope they enjoyed the Greek service. It strikes me that a little politeness would have been an equivalent in effect to the Greek service. But then we must not criticise our neighbors' religion. The Presbyterian remarked to me, with an awful sneer, that Mr. C—— and his companion had attended the Greek Mass and "gone through all the antics," which struck me as a very respectful characterization of religious movements, whether Protestant or Catholic. But then we are all uncharitable, and I am puzzled at times to find any one who is the least lenient in religious matters. The rest of the party survived the dreadful shock to our feelings by hearing a Presbyterian preach, in fact enjoyed his sermon, which admission I consider entirely magnanimous since neither of the Presbyterians went to hear me preach in Jerusalem. Of course that little fact they easily forgot, and, as I did not in the least care, I did not of course allude to it.

From the church we went to call on the minister, who has a large and roomy, although hardly a pleasant place of abode. From here we returned to the camp to reflect, and also to take our luncheon, which the Arab cook took especial pains to prepare. It seems strange that I remember that luncheon so well, while I have entirely forgotten the sermon. I wonder if ministers took as much pains to give people what they liked as cooks do, if they would not succeed better. No one will tolerate a poor cook, while a great many do poor ministers.

The point of the matter is, there is not much to be seen in Nazareth. The Latin Convent, the Greek Church, and the English Orphanage constitute the entire sum of sights. Possibly, it is owing to this fact that I enjoyed my day at this place so much. It is certainly a well-understood fact to travelers, that an absence of things to see is occasionally refreshing. Here we had only the place. Yet, was not that enough? Nazareth is now a large village, with, possibly, six thousand inhabitants. Of these there are only about two thousand Moslems, so that, to all intents and purposes, it is a Christian settlement. Raised up above the plain, it is still secluded among its own hills, nestling in the curve of one like a half-moon. One main street runs through it, which is narrow, but still much better than most Eastern streets. The houses are mostly of stone, substantial and solid. Within, the town is not attractive, but from without it is charming. After one has visited the Latin Convent and seen the spot where the Annunciation took place, and then visited the Kitchen of the Virgin, a mere cave, one is pre-

pared to be told how the actual house of the Holy
Family was carried off by angels to a spot on the
coast of Dalmatia, whence it was again carried to·
Loretto. There a church was erected, and a town
soon rose around it. Half a million pilgrims resort
to it annually. There is nothing in the Latin Convent to strike the attention, nor is there much to be
seen in the Greek Church of the Annunciation.
The Greeks have the better claim to the position,
simply because their tradition is the older. They
say that Mary was drawing water at the fountain
when the angel appeared to her.

The English Orphanage stands upon a hill just
without the town. As I have said, the beauty of the
place is in the environs. The basin set in here on
the top of the hills is not narrow, nor does it seem
shut in, but a good view from one hill-side sweeps
over the valley, and the appearance of the hill-tops
is not disagreeable. As one climbs up to the Orphanage, of course the valley lies out more plainly
in view, and from the building itself an extent of
land is seen, a little surprising to one who has viewed
the town only from the interior.

It may strike the careless, and perhaps the careful reader as well, that an orphanage in this land is
a little singular. The question naturally arises, why
should we support the orphans of the heathen? I
must confess I do not see. When there are millions
of Christian children crying out for a little help, it

certainly does seem preposterous to take the native Arab and educate her, for what? Simply for misery, that misery which must always follow one who is out of place. Yet the institution flourishes. Indeed, so long as English purses will pour their money into its coffers it must flourish. Orphans are extremely common, and all men will grasp opportunities and advantages. Why is my brother in the East End of London less worthy than these miserable beings who have not the instincts of truth or of civilization in them? Are these girls going back to their mud huts to live among the filth of their people? But the humanitarian, who is, I fancy, always more a sentimentalist than a man of sense, cries out that she will raise them. Raise them, I repeat. Go into their houses and see what a superhuman un dertaking it is to raise such a mass of filth. The only result must be that the girl either goes back to her old ways, or she leaves her home. Either course cannot be upheld by a Christian. In London, helped by all the arts of civilization, a girl may rise and hold her position, but here it seems so difficult. Yet it is by teaching that the missionaries maintain their hold. Says Doctor Geikie: " The people of Cana naïvely remarked to the missionary:

'Preaching is no use; give us schools.'" He adds: "'There are five stations in the villages around, but it would need the enthusiasm and self-denial of a St. Paul to do much real good, so stony and indifferent is the population, and so poor." I can only say again, Poor London! No wonder that foreign missions do not flourish when such a man as Dr. Geikie remarks upon the barrenness of the field. The expenses of the Orphanage, which maintains eighty-seven girls, must be considerably over a thousand pounds a year. While this is very cheap for the girls supported, it would keep five missionaries in London, who could do more good in a week than this institution, as admirable as it is in everything except its foundation, could do in a year. Yet I could not but be pleased with what I saw. Everything was delightfully clean and neat. The girls were happy, for the most part; indeed, they might well be. The situation was extremely healthy, high above the town, and far enough above the sea-level to be cool. The size and character of the place astonished me, and I could not but deplore the mistaken enthusiasm which could plant in a waste place such a power for good.

Perhaps the most agreeable part of our visit to this place was the cheerful, home-like feeling we had as we sat in the parlor and chatted with the teachers. Everything was English, and it was extremely refreshing to find in so strange a land the comforts of the West.

But we were on our way to the Wely Siman on the top of the hill behind Nazareth, where one of the best views of the country may be obtained. One thought must arise when once one stands upon this spot. Our Lord, not a child of ordinary intelligence, but with a mind filled with love for the people to whom He was sent, could hardly have failed to select this place from which to view the country which lay before Him in open panorama. The hours of meditation, when His mind was filled with thoughts which we can hardly comprehend, would be filled full, too full, indeed, as He gazed over this fair land which held the people who were to reject Him. The unutterable love, rising in his heart, would go forth over these broad plains to those whom, obstinate and sinful, He yearned to save. The thought of their cruelty could not quench this longing, and even then, while His mission was not yet begun, He would suffer the pang of coming sorrow.

And as we look, surely we too must have a little of that feeling, for, with the history of His life well in mind and the events which followed His death, we cannot but have a tinge of bitterness to think how such vast love for men could be so willfully rejected.

Esdraelon, softly green, yet fading into gray this beautiful spring after-

noon, is like some goddess stretched out there to
typify glorious and beautiful nature. The eye follows its graceful wavings, which add to the soft
beauty of its form, breaking yet not destroying the
effect. This is not some vast prairie which ends
with the horizon, but a plain whose gentle bil-
lows are like some summer sea, rolling into land,
because there is, I fancy, more beauty in the curved
than in the straight line. Then too the jagged edge
is a masterpiece from Nature's hand, for while it is
not sharp, it softly draws the line where the scene
should end. If the distance is blue and faint, it is
because the Judean Hills are far away. The clear
sky with greenish tint is mocking the blue, while
nearer come the hills of Carmel's range, rising darker
and darker until they stop with some emphatic pause
at Haifa by the Sea. The sun, which is all yellow
and gold, is winking a little as though almost ashamed
to create a beauty so divine, yet wondering perhaps
if the colors would be better should he plunge behind the Carmel range. So long as it lights up the
plain between, all before us is life. The dark sides
of the mountains fall into shadows which seem quite
appropriate to Elijah's memory, and his stern life is
far more real, because from where we stand there is
a grimness in the view of his most remarkable undertaking. We can see the Prophet that sunny day
so long ago, when no clouds were to be seen, and
all this fair land was burnt and seared by drought,

when this fierce man, who allowed no tampering with the religion he loved, sent his servant to look for a cloud. We almost instinctively seek for some cloud ourselves, but there is none ; no, not one the size of a man's hand.

Just under Carmel is Haifa, a pleasant town I am told, which threatens to become the port of the country, especially should a railway or a canal be made.

To the north lies Acre, but we can hardly see these places from where we stand. How often must our Lord have stood on this point and thought upon the history of His country, nay of His very ancestors. To the north almost behind our backs is Hermon, jewel of the East. Tabor stands alone rising a little jealously, I fancy, above all the hills, because Hermon is higher and more beautiful. The valleys around we have spoken of before, and it were but repeating were we to rehearse all the many famous things which happened within our gaze. It is almost too much. The mind is crowded with ideas, and a little talk about the old Moslem who was buried on this spot acts as a relief. The hills around look picturesque, trees are abundant, the rocks are covered, and the country is not so fearfully desolate as it was in Judea.

As we descended toward the town we had a good opportunity to view its situation, and to observe the long, straggling village, built against the side of the hill, as though mounting up, but not quite reaching the top. The white houses, somewhat gray with age or stained by the weather, were clustered in groups or stood isolated on the hill-side. Gardens around with trees gave a home-like aspect, such as one hardly sees in Palestine. Indeed, in all the Holy Land I have not seen another town which so well realized the English idea of comfort. The roads without the village were good as they led off into the country, the suburbs were pleasant, and the streets tolerably clean. There was an air of respectability about the place, which must certainly come from the presence of so large a Christian population. As we entered the village the people seemed more respectable, the filth, the squalor, so very prominent in most Eastern places, were wanting. As we came by the fountain, perhaps the very fountain from which Mary drew water, the women standing around formed a picturesque and not a

disagreeable sight. Their bright faces were handsome, and to this day the reputation of beauty is well
deserved by them. Thus did Mary stand many a
night chatting with her neighbors, her bosom swell-
ing with the consciousness that she
was the mother of the Messiah.
Did she understand then how much
future ages would adore her very
name? But she thought her son
was to be an earthly king. Even her
mother-love could not foresee how
great His name would be, and before
her very eyes He died an ignominious death.

Our tents were pitched quite near the fountain,
so that a row of urchins and a few adults formed
with the cactus hedge a kind of fringe around us,
which made, it is true, an interesting but hardly
agreeable sight. The servants were having a very
pleasant time this day, and were seated around chatting happily. Their costumes have for some time
been my study, and I have come to the conclusion
that a peasant's dress in this region consists pretty
much of chance pieces sewed together. In Beirût
or in Damascus there seems to be a fashion, but
here it is, perhaps, a lucky thing if one have cloth, I
will not say clothes enough, to keep one warm. One
woman, who stood near the tents, attracted my attention, because she had on her neck a coin similar

to one I had picked up in Jerusalem. The strange
thing about these coins is that they cannot easily,
indeed, I was told could not at all, be found in
Europe. The Austrian double ducat, worth ten
dollars, is, perhaps, the finest coin ever made. As
large as a silver dollar, it is much thinner, and is exquisitely cut, having on one side the arms of the
empire, and on the other the head of the emperor,
Francis II. The workmanship is as fine as any
jewel could be made, and in a country where jewelry
consists mostly of coins it is not strange that they
are in great demand.

This leads me to speak of some Cufic coins I got
at the same time. Long before the present Arabic

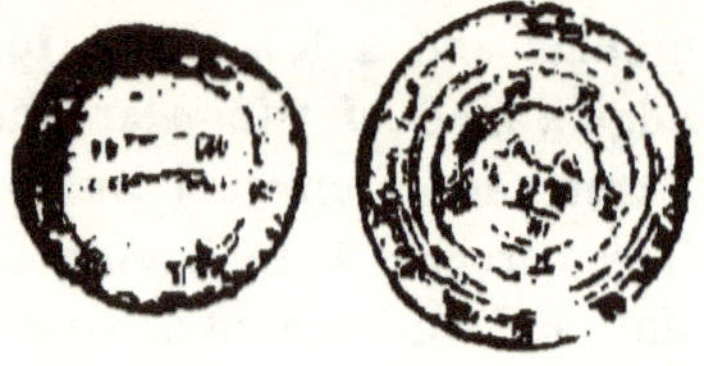

characters came into use the Cufic form was in
vogue. These coins are, therefore, of very great
age. One which I obtained was struck off soon
after the Hegira, probably some time during the
eighth century. The reason these coins have been
preserved to the present date comparatively unin-
jured shows how the Orientals horde their money.

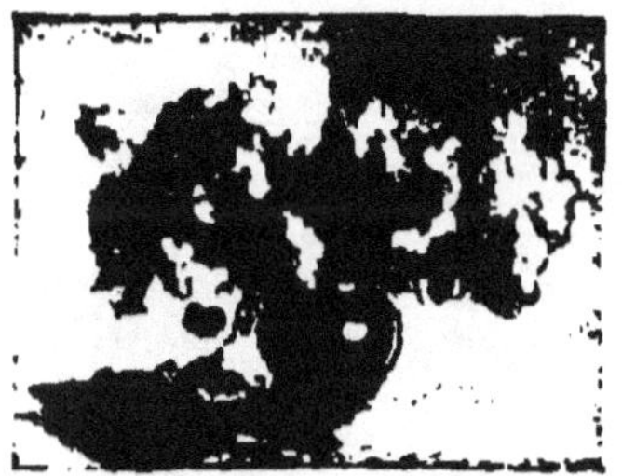

XVI.

The Sea of Galilee.

ALTHOUGH we were but one day's ride from the Sea of Galilee, where we were to take another day's rest, still I think we all felt disinclined to mount our horses and proceed on Monday morning. But necessity knows no law, and the trip was ordered to cover a certain amount of territory in a certain number of days. Consequently we had to push on, and had it been in a pouring rain we should have been obliged to move forward just the same. There is a certain sense of army discipline in the reflection that one must follow the dragoman, no matter what may turn up. I had of course provided myself with rubber coverings, which in case of wet weather would have completely covered me. A very kind friend in Rome, who had just been through the country, gave me long leggings, for he said they could not be purchased in the East. An overcoat I obtained in Cairo at a Jew store in the Mooskee. As the sign was in German I naturally spoke that language when negotiating for the article. Of course I refused to pay the price demanded, and the attendant turned to the head of the firm to know what he would take—speaking in Italian. He got his answer, and was greatly surprised when I offered him the same that he was told to get for it. These things, although being of no earthly use to me in my trip through the country, because we had no rain, might have been of inestimable benefit. When one has to face the onward march, no matter what it may be, there cannot be too much precaution. They tell me that it is almost death to be caught in a rain-storm without protection. Indeed it not infrequently happens that an unacclimatized person falls a prey to the fever thus brought on, and the sad death of two daughters of one of our college-presidents, some time ago, ought to be a sufficient lesson to compel people to care for themselves.

Yet Mr. and Mrs. W—— came to Jerusalem not expecting to go through the country, and then decided, quite unprepared as they were, to undertake the trip. Mrs. W—— was without a riding habit, and had to travel in her ordinary clothing, which was most disagreeable. Had it rained the conse-

quences of their carelessness might have been serious. It is not often that week after week will go
by at this time of year without some rain, so we
were especially fortunate that we escaped.

The ride from Nazareth takes one up among the
hills lying above the town, so that the view is very
interesting, as one looks for the last time upon the
quiet home of our Lord. Then plunging into the
defiles, or going over the long bare hills, we find
rough roads and only occasionally a fig or an olive
tree to enliven the scene. The little nest of comfort, which we have just left, stands quite alone
among these barren mountains. Not far off toward
the west is Seffurieh, which was, in the time of Josephus Sepphoris, the largest town in Palestine, and
after the destruction of Jerusalem the seat of the
Sanhedrim for several centuries. We then pass the
village of Reineh, which has nothing but an old
sarcophagus standing by the roadside, used for a
watering trough, to recommend it. The scenery is
extremely dull and the roads very bad. But soon
we ride into a hamlet, which like most Eastern
villages is composed of houses so low and so insignificant, that it is not until well in the town that
we are aware of the place. This is Kefr Kenna,
which they claim to be Cana of Galilee. However
there is very good reason to believe that another
village near Sepphoris, Kana el-Jelil, nine miles
north of Nazareth, may be the place. The name of

the latter is in its favor, but the position of the former seems more in accordance with the events which happened at Cana of Galilee.

There are, possibly, one hundred and fifty inhabitants, but, with the exception of the house where the marriage feast took place, there is very little which betokens prosperity. Not long ago one hundred and twenty Orthodox Greeks in this place became Romanists, and as a reward a Franciscan monastery is being built. If the inhabitants of Kana el-Jelil were only as keenly alive to the importance of their place they might gain a great deal of advantage. Indeed, perhaps b e f o r e long they will appreciate the benefit of booming their town, with such a good chance as they have for rivaling Kefr Kenna. Of course, the stone jars in which water was made wine are pointed out, and these constitute the only interest of the place. Around the

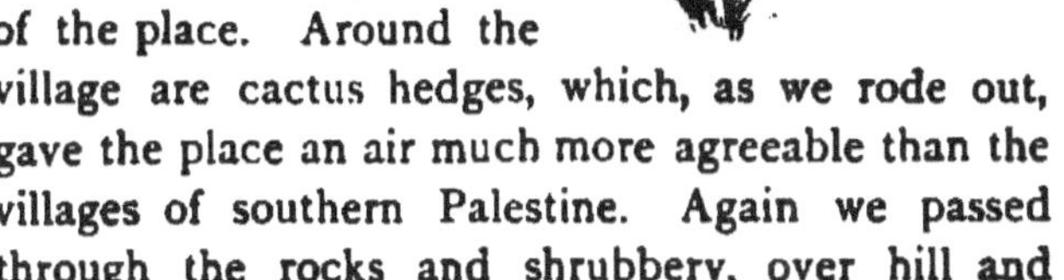

village are cactus hedges, which, as we rode out, gave the place an air much more agreeable than the villages of southern Palestine. Again we passed through the rocks and shrubbery, over hill and through valleys, until the monotony became very unpleasant. But the Philologist's wife varied it a little, for her horse in going down a slippery rock was not so cautious as the rest and lost its footing, so that it sat down suddenly. The lady, naturally, rolled off, and, as the place was quite steep, was only saved by the man riding behind, who, jumping from his horse, pulled her up and pushed the animal away, so that he was obliged to step in another direction when he recovered his footing. The party halted and after the excitement had subsided resumed its course.

Among these rocks and stones of Galilee the wild flowers grow with great luxuriance. Under the shelter of every boulder a great cluster of cyclamen hides its beautiful pink tints, as though withdrawing and blushing a little because of shyness ; not so the bright red anemone. This stands forth boldly all over the fields, causing some to appear a mass of color as the eye travels over the distance. Fences there are none, but occasionally the cactus will raise its prickly hedge, covering by its luxuriant growth great patches of ground. When planted in rows it soon becomes ten and even twenty feet in width.

After a time, however, the country improves, for we are leaving the rugged hills of Nazareth behind, and are coming into the plain which reaches down to El Buttauf. This is, in fact, a level table-land, which, with a little care, would teem with vegetation and plenty. But the robbers of the eastern districts beyond Jordan and the still greater robbers at Constantinople discourage any exertion. Lubieh stands on the top of a low, rocky hill, with fig and olive trees and rows of the prickly pear. Then we pass through a deserted but fertile country, until we come to the hill, which in the time of the Crusaders was considered to be the Mount of the Beatitudes. It is also related that here the five thousand were fed. It requires, however, but little reflection to see that the scene of the miracle must have been east of the Sea of Galilee.

But we have a better reason for lingering in this spot, for here the battle which sealed the fate of the Crusades was fought in 1187. For two days the battle raged among these slopes, but the enervated Christians were no match for the victorious Kurd, who burst upon them with his fifty thousand men, and, guided by a weak king, their follies came home to them at last. The vast undertakings which had planted a Christian kingdom in the heart of the Arabs fell, a worthy example of the weakness of vice and the selfishness of men. Guy de Lusignan retreated to the hills, but was taken prisoner with his followers, and soon after all the strongholds of the Christians yielded to the Moslem yoke.

17

Riding down the slope we come to a rich valley. A wide, deep glen opens before us, the country is still deserted, and we keep on, until at last we come out on the top of a hill, and the Sea of Galilee bursts on our vision. It is impossible to describe the first impression of this beautiful sheet of water. While there are no great mountains to mark it as distinctly picturesque, it has that quiet beauty which must come from soft atmospheric effects. They say it looks best from the heights when a thunder storm is coming up. It was not my fortune—I know not whether to call it good or ill—to see it under that advantage; but this sunny day, when the lake, one thousand feet below us, and the hills of Gaulinitis on the opposite side gave back to our gaze their own precious blue, I was compelled to pause and consider all that lay within my vision. Around was rough hill-side, descending or ascending, brown, yet somewhat tinged with green ; below, the sea ; beyond, the distant hills, each perfect in form, yet rising to a plain which stretched out far beyond my gaze ; to the south, the same wide reach of country going into the desert regions of the East ; beyond, far beyond my sight, lay, I knew, the land of the Chaldeans, Babylon, Nineveh, and the Euphrates River. The imagination roaming over that vast extent, which was, it is true, shut off by the nearer hills, takes no account of space, but ever stretches on like some electric spark, which spurns mere dis-

tance, as though of heavenly fiber.   Yet, as the eyes
sweep toward the north, there rises Hermon, sweet
signal of peace and purity to this dark land, with its
precious crystal sides, a veritable sign from heaven,
if the Pharisees had only seen it aright.   It is enough.
The one great thought that all this country lacks the
very purity which glitters from yonder peak is depressing, and slowly I urge Bucephalus onward, until
Tiberias comes in sight, placed
just at the edge of the water.

I named my steed Bucephalus

because, as some one suggested, it required a great
man to ride him.   The greatness consisted, I believe, mostly in patience.   No one in the party
could endure the thought of exchanging with me,
for they said they had not enough courage to make
him keep up with the rest.   But Bucephalus and
myself were beginning to jog on amicably by this
time, and I found out some of his weaknesses and
used them accordingly to aid my purposes.

Just outside the city stands a ruined castle, which is extremely strong-looking and gives evidence to the great power which once held this place. The walls of the city remain, but within there are dilapidated shanties, filled with nothing but filth and human beings. Past the castle and past the town we took our way, until we came to the beach beside the water. Our tents were already pitched a half mile from the town, so as to prevent too great intimacy with the inhabitants. Our journey was ended, and although the ride from Nazareth can be done in five hours, we had consumed a large portion of the day.

As the lake is six hundred feet below the level of the sea, we found the climate much warmer than on the hills. Luxuriant vegetation lined the shores and climbed a short way up the hills. Our camp was just away from the water's edge among some

low shrubbery and high grass. The sand beach in front made it a very pleasant spot. Our first impulse was to bathe in the clear, blue water, which lapped the shore so gently. The twilight was delightful, and the view in every direction charming. To the south stretched out the sea, until it was closed in by the hills beyond. Everywhere was the beautiful, blue water, gently sending its ripples on to the sand. But we remembered very well how fiercely these same waves tossed in times past, especially on that dark night when the disciples were far from land, toiling all night, yet unable to reach the shore. The figure of our Lord standing out in the darkness must have sent a thrill through their hearts. Then, when the impetuous Peter essayed to walk on the water, our Lord stretched forth His hand in calm majesty to raise him. It brings the scene very near to gently touch this same water, which can be so fierce, and yet, at times, so quiet. Surely on this tempestuous sea our Lord found a fitting type of the vicissitudes of His own life. One can scarcely realize the stirring events which had this place for their scene of action, or the wonderful things which were wrought by Christ's own hands around these shores.

The next morning after we had breakfasted, and found, to our surprise, that the tents were not struck, for the usual custom was to clear everything away as soon as possible, we sauntered down to the shore, where two boats were waiting for us. Indeed, this was an experience. We were to have a ship at our disposal. But as the party was not quite ready (some one is always late in a party of tourists), I sat down to sketch the little building erected by Ibrahim Pasha over the hot springs, about a mile below Tiberias. It is now falling into decay, but it looks well at a distance, and that was about all I cared for. Then we took up our small belongings, for, as we were to sail all day, we could afford to have something by us, and got into the " ships," as they call them in that region.   A boat, about

fifteen feet long and four or five wide, constitutes their idea of a ship.   The snub-nosed craft, the same at both ends, has no appliance for convenience, but seems made for the especial annoyance of the men who row.   The sides are twice as thick as are necessary, and the depth of it astonishing.   I fancy they are made to carry great loads of fish, and so must be bulky.   But with our party, which was divided among the two boats, there seemed to be very little water displaced.   Four men rowed and the drago-

man steered. I secured a seat on the rear deck, for
at either end there are small decks which serve as
seats, although, to be comfortable, it is necessary to
sit in Turkish fashion, as the feet will not reach the
bottom of the boat. There is place for a sail, but
we had no appliances for sailing on board, and I,
for one, was glad, for I fancy that with such a craft,
and with such skill as the boatmen possessed, a
squall would have caused us great danger.

As we left the shore we soon came opposite to

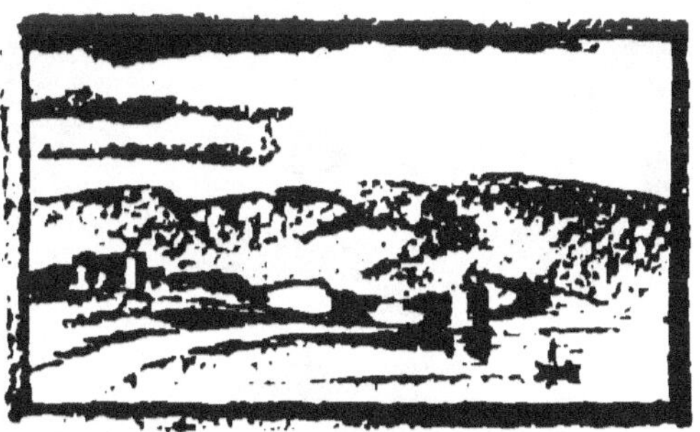

the city of Tiberias, which looks much more hab-
itable from the water than from the land. The sea-
wall was greatly broken down, and the city much
destroyed by the earthquake in 1837. Tiberias is
one of the sacred cities of the Jews, ranking after
Safed, Hebron, and Jerusalem. It seems rather
strange that it is so, for Tiberias was built by Herod
the " Fox," and was not, so far as we know, ever
entered by our Lord. The reason, doubtless, is
that in building it, a grave-yard was uncovered, and

the place was thus rendered ceremonially unclean. Thus all good Jews avoided it, and in order to have it peopled, Herod offered houses to freedmen, and even to slaves, to induce them to settle there. At present the Jews form nearly half the population, which is, all told, not more than 2,000. The city became a center of Jewish learning after the destruction of Jerusalem, and here the Mishna and the Jerusalem Talmud were completed.

The boats glided by the town, and the various

trades seemed going on in the lazy way so peculiar to the East, and soon we had gone beyond them and were looking to the north, where the most beautiful combination of mountains made its appearance. From the east and from the west the hills sloped down toward the sea, while in between rose Hermon, pale blue and tipped with a diamond crest, which flashed and flashed in the sunlight, until we were tired of gazing. It is in such things rather than in grand or regular beauty that the lake is attractive.

It is in the soft tints which bewitch the artist, rather than in the fine forms which boldly outline themselves against the sky, that one admires this place. It is the ever-changing water, which grows dark at one moment, light blue the next, glinting and gleaming in the sun, and the diamond star of Hermon over all. It is the ethereal blue of the eastern hills, the green touched with brown of the nearer mountains, which, softly blending, bring despair to one who seeks to make these things real on paper. When seen by the eye of some cold Biblical student these scenes are either extremely beautiful because associated with the learning he loves, or extremely commonplace because there is in his eye no room for color, or in his soul no place for poetry.

The Sea of Galilee is shaped like a pear, about twelve miles long and seven miles in the widest part. Thus as we sailed directly north we gradually drew out into the middle of the lake, with the Plain of Gennesaret to our left, and the hills of Gaulinitis to our right. One cannot but reflect upon the busy traffic which was constantly going on in the time of our Lord, when great cities lined the shores and all the pomp and circumstance of a kingdom was located at Tiberias. We are too apt to think that those days were much as we find the Holy Land to-day. But we must remember that all the arts of Rome, all the grace and learning of Greece, were pouring through this region and the ample ruins, ruins which are amazing as we look at them, prove the magnificence of that era. Our Lord was not a humble man teaching a rude people ; He was to all intents and purposes a laboring man who was rebuking the vices of a generation almost as accomplished, if far more wicked than the present. Whole fleets of boats were reflected in the waters, a navy and large commercial marine, if we can judge from the battle between Josephus and Vespasian.

To get an idea of the richness of the surrounding country and the wealth which was here located, with

the lake as a center, we have the towns Magdala, Capernaum, Chorazin, the two Bethsaidas, Gamala, Hippos, and Tarichea on the beach. Then in the surrounding country were other and larger cities, such as Scythopolis, Gadara, and Pella, besides numerous populous villages. To-day we see only Tiberias, a miserable village, in ruins for the most part. Thus the fame of Jesus could easily flash through this country, where nearly every foot of ground was teeming with population, and where great crowds could readily be gathered together. Besides, there was the wily " Fox " at Tiberias, also the Tetrarch at Banias to the north. Roman power and Roman wealth were constantly encouraging the arts, and to-day we can hardly liken the Sea of Galilee to anything but New York Bay, surrounded by cities. Of course there was, probably, no city of any very great size on the shores of the lake, but their number fully made up for their comparative smallness.

Our boats were heading for Tell Hum, situated on the northern coast. The ruins here, which have been thought by many to be ancient Capernaum, lie close upon the shore, and are interspersed with thickets and brambles. They cover a tract about a half mile long and a quarter of a mile wide. Great blocks of basalt prove the grandeur of former structures, and the magnificence of the ruins shows the importance of the buildings. One structure is seventy feet long and more than fifty feet wide. Within and without this place are strewn in great confusion capitals of columns, pieces of sculpture, ornamented friezes, and the like. The columns are large, but not long. These are supposed to be the ruins of the Synagogue, which, if this be the real site of Capernaum, may have been the very place where Christ spoke and read the Law. Some scholars think this Chorazin, while many place it at a distance two miles from the lake. The arguments for and against are so varied and so confusing, and withal so unsatisfactory, that it is hardly worth while to state them here. It is only interesting to reflect that, without doubt, these very streets were trod by our Lord, who had His home near this spot. Capernaum must have been within a short distance of these ruins, even if they be not the remains of that city whose pride reached unto heaven.

Not far from this place are more ruins, which are thought to be those of Bethsaida. Here was the home of Peter, James, and John. But there is nothing now to be seen, only a few ruins, a low marsh along the shore, and just in front of Bethsaida a sand beach. Lazily we drifted on, for the exertions of the men at the oars were not so strenuous as to cause us to move rapidly. Their bright eyes gleamed with a fire which little accorded with their indolent ways. It must be a matter of constant wonder to them why we go to this deserted spot to see a mass of stones. Indeed, if they knew how little the majority of these same travelers knew concerning these stones they would wonder more. I fancy they are themselves entirely ignorant of the history of their surroundings. Dr. Geikie relátes that the Sheikh of Samaria came to him to learn the history of that place.

So the boat went on, almost, as it seemed to us, without purpose, since we could only discover that we were skirting the shore, which is here edged with trees and shrubbery. At last, however, the order was given to land. We had had a whole day on the lake, and the experience was extremely pleasant. The boat was so primitive, so heavy, and so useless, according to our ideas, that one almost hesitates to believe that the boats were no better in the time of

Christ. But then fishing-boats were, doubtless, the same during all time, as clumsy and as common as possible. So that, doubtless, the same kind of ship carried our Lord over these same waters in His trips to and from the cities on the eastern coast of the lake. As we landed we found we were on the edge of the Plain of Gennesaret, which stretched away to the south for three miles. Beautiful grass and many low trees covered it, while around a small stream running into the lake high reeds shut out any extended view. To the south lay Magdala, the home

of Mary, while just at hand was Khan Minieh, by many people supposed to be the site of Capernaum. Here we found our tents pitched and our horses picketed around.

Just opposite the door of our tent was a high rock, and bursting forth from under it a stream of water. Near by was an ancient fig tree, from which the place takes its name, Ain-et-Tin. The spot was most attractive, perhaps as pretty in its quiet beauty as any we had seen. The soft browns and yellows of the rock, high enough to be a precipice, were mirrored in the transparent water. The reeds and grass around also had their counterparts in the smooth

sheet of liquid silver, while above them rose the
distant bluish-green of the mountains ; at our feet,
a few stones and soft, green grass. Just
within the inclosure stood the tents, and
the horses and mules were gathered
around. The servants were, for the

most part, silent, lying down to rest, although their
day's work had been light, since, while we were on
the water, they had only to come up the western
coast about seven miles and pitch the tents anew.
The cook, as usual, squatted down behind his little
charcoal stove, apparently doing nothing, but occasionally looking into a little oven, and at times stirring what was to appear afterward as soup. I
never saw less trouble for so great results. Seated

in one spot, he seemed to have everything within reach, and the calm smile on his brow was never interrupted by disappointment because his preparations had not been productive of excellent food. Around him we gathered as good genii, not, I trust, because we worshiped the gastronomic art, but because so genial was his countenance, and so homelike his tent, that we felt perfectly satisfied to watch him, even if we could only express our ideas with a smile. It has struck me that Cook, who has been so eminently successful in the tourist business, sends along first-class cooks, and neglects to be particular about the dragomans, because he has so many ministers in his parties. If so, he is a clever man.

Yet the cook could not take all the attention, for our Presbyterian friend from Pennsylvania was always talking about his wife, and we unmarried men felt just a little jealous, and also a bit amused, when we heard him call other ladies "dear." Such was doubtless the force of habit. I never hear a man talk affectionately about his wife, but I have a longing to see her. We had by this time become quite well acquainted, and the party had settled into terms of mutual forbearance. It seems that wherever people get together they form into cliques. The widow being the only unmarried lady with us, there could hardly be room for the usual petty jealousies, since the two married ladies kept strictly under their husbands' wings, protected and guided by them in all matters.   Indeed Mr. and Mrs. W—— seemed to prolong their honeymoon, and cling to it with great pertinacity. The Philologist and his wife were more interested in reading than the rest, so that the un-married men were left much to themselves, although of course there was always the widow in case of too much ennui. The reverend gentleman from Penn-sylvania was endeavoring all the time to take the rit-ualism out of Mr. C——, but had, I fear, very hard work. His one great argument was the widow, of whom he did not approve, and Mr. C——, who was a little fond of the same lady, became at last very much mixed up in his mind. Hilton and myself were of course greatly amused, while the traveled American, who was so obstinate, and so sure he did not snore, took but a languid interest in anything.

So we were well prepared to undertake the long journey over Mount Hermon, which is, I should say, entirely unnecessary. I should advise any one going independently to proceed with Cook's party so far as Nazareth, and then to leave the country at Haifa. From Nazareth one could easily take an excursion to Tiberias and the Sea of Galilee and return. Then if he desire to see Damascus and Baalbek, which he really ought not to miss, he could enter the country again at Beirût, thus avoiding that tedious tramp through the mountains. But we did not, of course, understand how tiresome we should find it. At first camp life seemed delightful. At the Jordan it

was perfection.   Indeed while coming up through
the country there was every pleasure and few draw-
backs in it.   But after we left Nazareth we began to
get tired.   It was, in fact, an old story.   Up to this
point we really enjoyed the trip.   After that we
began to grow weary.

Before leaving this place it would be well to state
that Dr. Robinson maintains with great ability that
this was the site of Capernaum.   The principal evidences in its favor are that it stood on the edge of
the Plain of Gennesaret, while Tell Hum is two
miles away from it.   Then the Plain of Gennesaret
was watered by "a most fertilizing fountain called

Capharnaum."   The fountain called Ain-Tabigah,
situated somewhat to the east of Ain-et-Tin, is likely
to be identical with the one Josephus mentions.
An aqueduct still remains which brought water to
the plain.   Thus perhaps it was here that our Lord

dwelt, and not at Tell Hum. Yet it does not so much matter, for it is certain that through this beautiful scenery, adorned by every grace of a great civilization, He wandered and taught those who followed Him the great truths by which we live at present. Here He must have passed, even this very spot. The ruins around, although now hidden by profuse foliage, were then palaces or buildings of pretension. The Plain of Gennesaret spreading out before us in loveliness, was so near His home that He could not have failed to pass through its lanes. Around are the very hills He once gazed at, which He even climbed in search of solitude, to get away from the throng which always followed Him when He made His appearance.

Surely the Sea of Galilee is a sacred spot, the one region so small in itself which saw so many mighty works. Even more than Jerusalem, which, although the center of Jewish faith, was hardly the center of wealth, this lake is consecrated by His footsteps, who here led years of happy life before He went up to be crucified. And it seems fitting that He should take the place of all Palestine which was most advanced in worldly wealth as His field. He went among men who desired help, those who were perhaps sinful and vicious, yet willing to do better and accept a nobler teaching than any they had yet had. And so the night, spent almost in the place which had heard the sound of His voice, became particularly impressive. In the night-watches it was easy to return to that ancient time, and people again this region with those who followed and heard the Lord Jesus.

XVII.

Over Mount Hermon.

THE road from Khan Minieh is as direct a contrast to the richness and beauty around the Sea of Galilee as can well be imagined. Starting from the smooth green sward, almost at once we found ourselves among rocks and stones which made our progress almost an impossible problem. The abruptness of the hills just in this region reminds one of the rocks around the Dead Sea. Indeed as both places are of volcanic formation, it is not strange. Not far from here among these fastnesses the Jews hid themselves in the caves, and defied for a long time the power of the Roman Government. But Herod, baffled so long by them, let down huge baskets or boxes filled with soldiers, and a fierce contest was waged in mid air. Finally the soldiers prevailed and armed with poles furnished with hooks they pulled out the robbers and threw them over the precipice. Once gaining a foothold they found sufficient stuff to make a fire, and so, filling the caverns and passage-ways with smoke, forced the inhabitants to yield. One man threw over his wife and children, and finally himself, in his despair. Indeed those must have been stirring times, even when the country was so well peopled. It seems almost strange that the same caves are not used now by robbers.

While the roads had been extremely bad over the distance we had come, they were not to compare with those we passed while crossing the mountains lying to the north of the lake. At one place, to aggravate the difficulty, the rock, evidently very soft, had been worn in the place called the road into holes, into which the horse stepped for a depth of two feet. It was quite a mystery to me why Bucephalus did not break his legs. Indeed, I fancy that the sagacity shown at this time so raised him in my estimation that I forgot his many failings. So the animals plunged on, each rider fearing that the next moment would find him lying a corpse by the wayside. The unpleasant thought about traveling in this country is, that, if one be thrown, or be otherwise injured, there is no way he can be cared for. A physician cannot be had, and carrying a sick person for a distance would be sure death.

Just to the east on the hill lay the famous city of Safed, one of the spots sacred to the Jews, and the place where a great deal of their learning and many of their scholars flourished in earlier days. A great castle rises above the town, from which a splendid view of the surrounding country can be obtained. It is supposed that this was " the city set on a hill " to which Christ alluded. From this point there are two roads to Banias, for which we were aiming. The one leads directly to it, taking two days to accomplish the journey, and the other takes three days, passing around among the hills. We were led the shorter route, for which, I think, no one felt the least regret.

From the top of the hill we got a last view of the part of the Holy Land which we had been examining, and then we turned our eyes northward away from sacred things to a country, perhaps, more beautiful, but not so interesting. Thus we found that passing through the long defiles over rocks and stones, riding for the mere sake of getting over the ground, was tiresome in the extreme. The ground, however, which filled up the spaces between the stones was very fertile, the grass and thistles coming up to the horses' bridles. The hills, covered with a wild herbage, seemed extremely picturesque at times, but very dreary and dull at others. Houses and villages were almost entirely wanting, but here and there we caught glimpses of the deep valley through which the Jordan flows, and this gave promise of something better soon to follow. At last we gained a point where Mount Hermon rises well above the hills, and with this for a guiding star we cheered up a bit. So we came to the foot of the mountains and skirted them, finding the road much better, yet not going very fast, because the ladies of the party could not ride rapidly. However, the younger members struck off for themselves when we reached a level stretch, preferring to gallop a little, even if we had to wait afterward for the party to catch up with us.

Hilton had named his horse Baalbek. When asked why he did so, he replied, "Because he is a great ruin." These horses were certainly an interesting study. It was remarkable the speed which could be got out of an animal which, at first sight, seemed only fit for destruction. Yet Baalbek, as Hilton humorously called him, would  stretch out his legs and speed across the plain at quite an astonishing rate. My own Bucephalus lacked ambition, but it was my especial duty, indeed, I might almost add my only occupation, to make him go. His disposition caused him to lag behind the rest, even when they were walking. At first I assumed this to be weariness caused by his misfortunes, but a more intimate acquaintance with him proved it to be laziness. I had secured a riding-whip at Jerusalem, with which I expected to cope with my difficulties, but I soon found that the horse looked upon that only as a kind of aggravation, without supposing for a moment, apparently, that it was intended to be an instrument of torture. I would, at times, use this whip across his flanks, with the only result that he stopped and kicked. Certainly, this was discouraging. I then borrowed of the dragoman, who seemed to be the general lender of the party, a spur, with which I tortured one side, and when the foot on that side became tired from too much exertion I put it on the other. By this means I accomplished two objects. I succeeded in getting through the country, and also in acquiring a great deal of exercise other than horseback-riding. If I added that I acquired patience, I fear some of my companions would rise up and dispute me.

The spot selected for our luncheon was extremely picturesque. Just before us was a natural reservoir, which supplied water for a mill, while stretched out before us was the plain, which lay between us and the hills on the other side of the Jordan. Mount Hermon stood forth in all its grandeur, plainly visible from base to summit. The brown sides, with its long seams running up to the snow-covered top, took their rise in the green of the plain, which was now gaining strength of color as the spring progressed. Just in the cut below the mountain, which separated it from the adjoining hills, lay Banias, our objective point. From the position we had taken it seemed no great distance across. But we were obliged to go up far to the north so as to cross the river, which, although not wide, is very hard to approach, because it is so surrounded by marshes. In front lay the Lake of Huleh. It is about four miles

long and a little more than three wide. All around it extend marshes and thickets of canes. It is just on the level of the sea, and thus more than six hundred feet above the Sea of Galilee. On either side are wide fields of fertile ground, cultivated partly by Bedouin sheikhs and partly by merchants of Damascus. It was to this region Herod came when young to kill the game which here abounded.

In this district the great battle was fought which gave northern Palestine into the hands of Joshua. When he captured Ai he found nearly all central Palestine at his mercy, but the northern portion stood defiant under Jabin, King of Hazor. Near by was the home of Barak, who with Deborah led the Hebrews in the great battle of Mount Tabor.

The rest here, although it was getting along in the afternoon, gave me time to finish a sketch of Hermon, which rose so majestically before us. Indeed, I doubt if it is so imposing from any other standpoint. From other places it rises over other mountains, but from this spot it stands naked and alone, like some huge giant, who stands with his muscles well developed, a very god for his beauty and his strength. While the mountain loses much by a near view, it gains in grandeur. The delicate shades are wanting, hard brown and gray rock predominate; but the snow on the top is ever glistening, pure and white as when first we espied it from the plain near Shechem. To linger here was to spend a most enjoyable hour. Not often does such a beautiful view stand out before one, or the rich plain below contrast so magnificently with the towering mountain above. The reds and browns, which mingled with the greens of the vegetation, seemed almost fiery in their glow, and the soft gleaming of the water, where the luxuriant vegetation appeared, was most delightful.

However, we had to ride a little farther, but as it was only along this beautiful plain, we had charming scenery at our side and a good road beneath us. So the hours passed pleasantly, enlivened by the merry chat of our companions or occupied by contemplation of that which was before us. Scattered along the plain were several tents belonging to the Bedouins, who come to these rich fields in spring and add to the effect of the place by their really picturesque dwellings. The long, black cloth is on one side erected on poles, and on the other fastened to the ground. If privacy is desired, another cloth is stretched across the front, and thus a tent, not very high, but quite good, is made, which, during the warm weather, must be comfortable, but, during a rainy spell, miserable. In front of the tents, for there are generally several grouped together, are numerous children, with men and women sitting

around, all perfectly idle. I do not think I ever saw a Bedouin do anything. Their brown faces, intelligent as a European's, seem not at all in accordance with their lazy habits. Perhaps a horse or two may be standing by, but they seemed scarce, and I fancy the boasted Arab steed is greatly a matter of fiction. Our camp was pitched on a level piece of ground, near a stream by which were a few men laboring. They were not, I fancy, what are known as Bedouin, but peasants hired by the owner of the soil. This spot was the most home-like and prosperous we had yet seen. The soil was magnificently fertile. The hills were some distance away, and around were many tents, showing their black sides above the vegetation along the bank of the stream. We arrived before ours were erected, and I was very tired, for the severe ride we had had over the mountains had been more tedious than any we had yet experienced. The sun began to get down below the hills, and, while it was delicious before it disappeared, the air was extremely chilly after it had gone. The twilight soon faded into gloom, and we were glad to sit around the cook's tent to get a little heat from his small stove. The ride had been one of such length, for the dragoman wished to get well upon our way to Banias, that the servants were behindhand in their work, and it was very dark before the welcome sound of the horn called us to dinner.

The next morning a ride of less than an hour brought us to Tell-el-Kady, the Hill of the Judge, the Dan of Scripture. Here is the site of the ancient city. At the western base the waters gush forth in great abundance, seemingly an underground river which here comes to the surface. One is amazed to see such a volume of water coming from the ground. It is probably the largest spring in Syria and the principal source of the Jordan. Around are trees, some large, others small, but altogether forming a beautiful grove, fresh and delightful. The wonderful clearness of the water, which is doubtless only the result of the snows on Mount Hermon which find an underground channel, cannot fail to please the eye. One almost hesitates to leave this beautiful spot, yet we had to press on, and rode through a charming landscape, thickly sprinkled with dwarf oak intermixed with hawthorne, oleander, and myrtle. Before us rose the heights of Hermon, while nearer the castle-crowned summit by Banias claimed the attention.

Crossing the picturesque bridge over the Hasbany we found parties of Arabs, who rode up to us in an expectant manner, and then we learned that Prince Charles of Sweden was just behind us, and this party were those attending the Swedish consul at Sidon, who had come out to meet the Prince on his way to

Damascus. A fine Arab horse attracted my attention, as he stood with his lordly neck and head raised sniffing the air. His rider, a true son of the

desert, must have been a man of circumstances to possess so fine an animal. I could not but observe that the horse needed proper feeding, for it was evident that he had only the rough care which one would naturally expect from the nomadic life his master led. The true Arab horse, which people who have not seen the real animal like to imagine,

is certainly a myth. In Cairo I visited the stables of the Khedive to find only English thoroughbreds. As we progressed we saw many more people, and at last came up to the Swedish consul himself, who was waiting patiently under a tree. It was disputed for some time whether we should have our lunch there or press on to Banias. At last Leighton decided that it was better to go on, and we soon rode into the town, which was not far distant from this point.

We found a camping-ground in a large olive plantation near the town, close by the spot where the Banias River rushes forth like a full-grown man who spurns to be a child. Around are evidences of ruin, and amid them stand the few houses which make up the modern village. The torrent of the Banias rushes out from under a precipice a hundred feet high, and over it is the cave which gave the name to the ancient city Paneas. A magnificent temple stood on this spot, and a *wely* still remains up on the top of the cliff. The Romans and Greeks found here a suitable home for their god Pan, and the inscriptions on the face of the rock tell the story of the place.

The origin of the town is shrouded in obscurity. Under Herod the Great the city became historic. After he accompanied Augustus to the sea he returned and erected a fine temple to him at a place called Panium. Afterward it became part of the territory of Philip, who rebuilt and enlarged it, and called it Cæsarea, in honor of Tiberius Cæsar, adding Philippi to distinguish it from Cæsarea on the coast. But the name Paneas became too deeply impressed upon the minds of the people, and it descended in the Arabic form Banias. It was in this city, or within this region, that our Lord asked Peter whom he thought Him to be. After this the Transfiguration took place, without doubt on one of the high peaks of Hermon, rising above the town.   After our luncheon, which we had near the place where our camp was to be pitched when the caravan came up, we remounted our horses and set out to visit the castle of Subeibeh, which rises so grandly above the village.   Off to the southwest the Jordan runs through a beautiful wilderness of trees and over picturesque rocks, while near at hand on the other side the gushing fountain remains a source of wonder as we look at it.

The bridge is very dilapidated, built of antique pillars minus the capitals, and is defended by a

large square tower.   Everywhere there is rushing water which spreads itself into little streams amidst the luxuriant vegetation.   We passed out of the town into the country and began to climb the mountain, which was exceedingly steep although planted quite up to the castle with olive orchards.

At last we gained a small level place at the east end and then, by going a short distance along the wall, we managed to gain an entrance with some difficulty into the ruins themselves. As one stands upon one of the western towers he must be astonished at the massive strength of the structure. Even in the present age, when the fortresses of antiquity are apt to appear puny, one must be struck with the extraordinary extent and splendid position of this fortress. It is a quarter of a mile long by nearly three hundred feet in width and makes no small walk from one end to the other. Great stones, ten and twelve feet long, show the skill and energy of the builders, while huge cisterns, whose gloomy depths in the vast towers are thrilling, testify to the great size of the garrison in time past. The whole is perched up fifteen hundred feet above Banias, and one is surprised to read that the scholars are not disposed to place its erection at a period earlier than the eighth century. It seems strange that so vast a monument, one grander than any Europe can show of a date nearly so remote, stands almost unknown, testifying to the great industry and the power of some prince in an age at which we are disposed to sneer. The ruins of the Rhine, wanting both strength and grandeur, appear puny beside this. The view from the western end

19

is superb, and is, I believe, considered one of the grandest in Syria. Far away are the hills of Galilee; below, stretched out like a panorama, is the plain of Hûleh, while all around are the slopes and out-lying hills of Hermon. After a couple of hours spent in wandering over the ruins, a time deeply absorbing yet unsatisfactory because we could learn nothing of their history, we returned, each going his own way

under the delusion that any one could go down a hill. This was emphatically true in some respects, but threatened to bring Hilton and myself into very great difficulties. While it was perfectly possible to get down a hill, the problem in our minds also included that of accomplishing the feat without breaking our necks, to say nothing of the necks of the valiant steeds we rode. When we almost deemed the case hopeless a way opened, and we found ourselves on familiar ground, happier by far because we had surmounted difficulties than those who had merely followed the dragoman.

The rest of the day was idly spent, for there was nothing more to see. I collected a few wild flowers which thrust up their pretty heads as if in mockery, almost daring me to sketch them. The rest of the party helped the cook by their silent admiration, and spoke as the spirit moved them. This was indeed a lazy life. At least it had been, but we were to cross the mountain on the morrow, and, I fancy, each and every one shrank from this as a species of torture. The poetry of camp-life was fast dying out. The obligation to pack up one's things every morning was becoming a hideous dream, so that if one were not so tired as not to sleep, there would have been some dreadful tales of nightmare. But the night season was marked as it had been before by the braying of the donkeys. The awful sound at first would startle us as though we had heard the howl of some wild beast. An angry word in Arabic accompanied by a kick would silence the animal. At times when the poor beast tried to make a sound I have seen such an expression of disgust come over its face when Leighton administered the necessary punishment, that I could not help laughing.

The ascent of the mountain the next morning was especially dreary. The road was bad and very steep, and although there were trees and a few houses along the way, it was still very uninteresting, becoming more so after we left Mejdel, a Druse village with industrious inhabitants. The country was bleak but still under cultivation. Hermon rose at our left hand, bare, and with its valleys filled with snow. The nearer view was not so enchanting as the first glimpses we had of it. Indeed, this is, I fancy, the case with most strong and great characters. All the morning we were climbing and did not begin to descend until afternoon, when, going rapidly down a very steep slope, we saw a village opposite us across a small stream, the houses of which clung to the cliffs. The stream, running with gentle murmur past the village, formed one of the two main tributaries of the ancient Pharpar. As we came down the slope, almost fearing our horses would stumble and thus bring us in some haste to the bottom, we saw the inhabitants of the village coming out to meet us. Leighton rode on ahead to learn if we might have water, I really do not know why, and we were soon surrounded by a crowd of Arabs, who could hardly be called admiring, because they evinced a wicked desire to annoy us. As the horses stood clustered together, and we were near by, the crowd pressed too close to be comfortable. The orders of the servants did not cause them to withdraw, so Mr. C——'s dragoman used his whip. This is generally the best and most satisfactory way of driving them off, but now it only roused their ire, and there promised to be some interesting episodes to put in our notebooks, supposing we lived to do it. But Leighton came back at this juncture, and a few conciliatory words or threats, I really do not know which, settled the matter, and we proceeded down the stream, seeking for a suitable place to take our luncheon. After we had got, as we supposed, the spot, we dismounted and prepared to rest, for we were very tired. But we were forced to move on, for groups of children and lazy fellows from the village came to annoy us, and we took up another position in a narrow gorge farther down the stream.

The scenery was very wild, and the rocks and stones together with the clay banks of the stream made a rather fierce picture, which our little experience with the inhabitants of Beit Jenn greatly heightened. When we were nicely ensconced in our new place, being together in misfortune, we became chatty and friendly. Mr. C——'s dragoman vouchsafed certain facts about his household affairs which greatly interested us. He had recently married a young girl of whom he was very fond. The household matters, everything, were detailed with perfect frankness, and in a way

which gave us a glimpse of the home life of a true
Arab.

We follow the stream until it unites with the
Sabirâny, and thence is known as the Pharpar. So
we turn to the left and skirt the base of the mountain and find ourselves, after a tedious day's riding,
at Kefr Hauwar. The rest is welcome and the village, surrounded by gardens and orchards, is pleasant. A little impatience began to possess, us for we

were only a few hours' ride from Damas-
cus, and pressing on, the next morning,
over a plain which descends gradually,
we reach a dreary desert in which we see
only a few tufts of grass ; but gradually
we approach a green paradise and get
glimpses ahead of a sea of verdure dotted
with white villages. The long gallop
over the wide stretch, with the mountains
rising grandly behind us, is in many respects agreeable. But the distance is
much greater than we imagined, for the
beautiful green oasis is, we are well aware, the
Damascus we are seeking. At last we come to some
trees, which form the dividing line between the
desert and the rich plain. Tradition places at this
spot the conversion of St. Paul. Leighton says we
are to take our luncheon here, but we rebel—in vain,
however, for we must dismount and eat. Our horses
are tied to the trees, and under their shade, which

is very welcome, for the sun is hot, we hastily eat the cold chicken, the canned meats, the bread and all the other stuff, which from two weeks' continued eating we have long since begun to hate. Indeed at one time my detestation of cold chicken was so great that I wondered if I could ever recover from it.

At last we are permitted to ride on and see this wonderful city, this paradise of the East. The country grows richer and richer, the trees more and more numerous, and the houses scattered around give a lovely picture of prosperity. Canals are frequent, carrying water to the plain, the real source of this fertility, and soon we find ourselves in what looks like a village, and which has some semblance to a village street. We are met by a beautiful Arab boy who has ridden out to meet us, partly to see his father who is the muleteer, and partly to learn if this is the Prince's party. He rode by all of us, his sweet full face bright with happiness, managing a much better steed than the one the muleteer vouchsafed me. By this time the whole party became a little anxious to see the great city, and we all rode rapidly along the wide street, with a canal by our side which is part of the Abana.

The magnificence of the East appears, the white houses, the quaint dresses, men on horseback, all together without order, yet exceedingly attractive, because it is once more the life of the city, from which we have been for some time absent. With what pleasure do we alight at the hotel and mount to our rooms, to live for a few days the life of civilization again. The cool rooms of the inn, the clean beds and the comforts of a hotel, even if it be a hotel in the East, ah! no one can understand them until he has had two whole weeks of hard riding and tent-life.

XVIII.

The Pearl of the East.

IT is impossible to describe the sensation of delight with which I entered the hotel. The very fact that I was in the " Pearl of the East," the paradise of Arabic writers, was enough. But then the hotel, although it was not Dimitri's, in itself a great disappointment, was rather romantic after one had recovered from a sensation of anger. We mounted a long flight of steps, and found ourselves in a beautiful large hall paved with marble and ornamented with columns. Divans were at either end, and the high windows let in a most refreshing breeze, which served to keep this vast apartment cool, and, at the same time, warm enough, so that we felt no chill. The climate was delicious, unlike anything we experience in America, unless sometimes in June we have a day in which heat and cold are mixed, in that delightful proportion with which one combines lemon and sugar to form a drink which shall be neither sweet nor sour. The great, cool room was so unlike anything we had before seen that it made us feel that for the first time we had met with the magnificence of the East. In Cairo, Shepheard's Hotel is large and comfortable, but is in no sense elegant.

I mourned for Dimitri's in spite of my pleasant quarters. There is something historic about that place, even if old Dimitri is dead and his widow reigns in his stead, which would have been extremely attractive. Besides that hotel is an old Damascene dwelling with courts, and divans in recesses, fountains, and the like. Here we were in a large, square building, which might have been erected in Italy, for all the semblance it had to an Eastern dwelling. At any rate, if Cook would insist upon sending us to the Victoria instead of Dimitri's, we might, at least, go and see the place. Leighton could not deny us that privilege. I think I waxed more angry when I learned that the Prince was to go to that hotel, for this gave Leighton a flat contradiction, since he had said the Victoria was the better of the two. If so, why, pray, did not the Prince come where we were?

Outside the sun was shining with that beautiful bright light, which, at this early period of spring, had not become a glare, so that everything smiled as we left the doorway to enter the town. The rushing river in front of us was what a sentimental writer would call pure gold, that is, it was the exact color of mud, and I could not but reflect that Naaman need not have used such a lofty tone about Abana and Pharpar rivers of Damascus, as though they were so much better than the Jordan. While he was quite right about their being as good as the Jordan at its mouth, he surely could not have gone down into Palestine by the way of Banias, or he would never have told such a glaring falsehood. While it is nice to be poetic, and very disagreeable to be too plain and straightforward, a fault into which few writers on this country fall, I must confess the prevailing aspect of every-thing I saw was good, yellow mud. The streets were of mud, dried, the water of the same shade, the houses of mud also, dried, and the vegetation a sickly green. But then there was the yellow sunshine, which was not mud, and the bright faces and fascinating dresses of the natives, plenty of life; a great deal which was of interest, busy traffic, camels, donkeys, horses, and scarcely a European. The charm of the place lay in the fact that it was so far away from civilization. Here, for the first time, I got the true flavor of the Orient. In Cairo there are wonderful things to be seen, but a quarter of the population are Europeans or Arabs dressed in the Frank costume. Here the Frank costume was rare. The Arab gentlemen dressed in their own picturesque garb. The Oriental reigned supreme. Besides, there was more real life, more sociability, and not such a rush as at Cairo. The city had no new glaring European buildings, which were either half-built or half-ruined. While too much care is not taken with the houses, they still have a more finished appearance and give a much better effect than in other places. The grouping of the houses, the minarets of the mosques, with the palms here and there, made pictures which at Cairo, I am sorry to say, they did not.

A long avenue led away from the hotel, the one down which we had just come. On either side were trees, luxuriant with foliage, birds were singing, natives were chatting. Dr. Geikie says he looked for something respectable, but was ever disappointed. Charles Dudley Warner says, " Damascus is simply a damp spot." These opinions from such eminent men crush me into insignificance, for I was more charmed with it than with anything I had previously seen. The one must have had a cold, and the other forgotten the necessary attendants of an Oriental city. I did not look for grandeur, I did not seek for a dry place, I was satisfied if I could only have the eye gladdened by a little color, a little of artistic form, a little harmony, and be relieved from that awful jumble of everything one sees elsewhere in the East. In short, I did not have the malaria, and was not afraid of water. I liked it, even if I could not say with enthusiasts that it was liquid gold. Just beyond the hotel across the river and its walls of stone, which keep it within bounds, is the citadel, with the soldiers lounging around in front, for the city gate is near by, and crowds of people gather around as though this were a general lounging place for the inhabitants of the city. The open square near the hotel is used as a horse-market, and although at this hour there were few people in it, still at times it presents quite a busy appearance.

We entered by the gate, passing groups of curious people ; for here the Frank is only an occasional visitor, and found inside a street which, although not wide, had considerable pretension for the East. A large bath-house stood on the right, shops were scattered all around, camels, donkeys, and Arabs disputed the way. Here, indeed, the scene was truly Oriental. While there was no grandeur, there was certainly a respectability in Damascus which one seeks in vain in other Eastern cities. The houses, while built of mud, have a soft whitish-yellow appearance ; the bright dresses, not so tattered and shabby as is usual, made a fascinating picture. The life was strictly Eastern ; no carriages as I could see, threatened passers-by ; there were only foot-passengers, or, perhaps, occasionally a horse-man.

Our objective point was Dimitri's, for I insisted that Leighton take us there at once to see if it were not more attractive than the Victoria. We passed down a street which seemed almost deserted, but comparatively clean. Indeed, where a certain writer saw all the filth in Damascus, I cannot im-

agine. Although Eastern cities are never very clean, still this place appeared to me remarkably free from the usual nastiness which seems to pervade the very atmosphere of the East. A low door, scarcely large enough to admit a stout man, was the entrance to this famous hostelry. Accustomed as I was to surprises, I could not repress an exclamation when I entered and found a delightful courtyard within. The ground was paved with marble, and the sides of the court, which was quite large, were black and white stone in stripes. In the center was an octagonal fountain playing in a style which brought vividly to the mind the Alhambra and the Arabian Nights, while to the left opened a wide recess, surrounded by luxurious divans. Papers, pipes, and a few chairs gave it a home-like aspect. A staircase led to the upper stories and roof, and vines and a little shrubbery finished the picture, which was in every way most charming. Leighton turned to know if the Victoria were not better, and I answered with so positive a "No" that he laughed. I also added that Cook sent us to that out-of-the-way place because it was cheaper. I afterward learned that the landlord of the Victoria was under great obligations to Cook, and had made a contract with him to take his "menagerie" at a certain reduced price. It was fortunate for us that we found the hotel empty, for otherwise we might have fared very poorly, it being the custom to neglect Cook's parties.

From Dimitri's we go to the bazaars. These seem far more extensive and better kept than those of Cairo. While the traffic does not appear very brisk, there is a dignified air about them which we could not find in other places. Great lines of shops, running through narrow streets, intersecting like a net-work at times, and growing more spacious and important as they line the street called Straight,

continually attract the eye. The different trades
have each their quarter, and the street, which is
covered over, affords a pleasant place to
walk. The Arabs seem more dignified and
less anxious to sell than most we have met.
The articles are quite the same as one would
see in any large Eastern city. The cop-
persmiths' bazaar shows rows of beautiful
red ware, while the shoe bazaar displays red
slippers, and in another quarter we come
upon great piles of common calicoes such as
we would despise in this country, but which
attract these people because of their gay
colors. So with every kind of article, each
is to be found in its appropriate quarter.

At one end of the street we saw a Bagdad donkey. It was pure white and much larger than the
other donkeys. An elaborate pattern was cut on
his flanks, as though the owner thought that his
appearance was not otherwise sufficiently attractive.
His saddle and all the appointments were of an
order which betokened the wealth of the rider.
Indeed only men of prominence have this kind of
donkey. Probably it bestows the same kind of dis-
tinction as a footman in livery.

The extent of the bazaars is something fatiguing
to one who goes in them only to see. The articles
look somehow commonplace when there is no one
trying to drive a sharp bargain. The true charm of

Oriental buying must lie in the bickering, the little manœuvres of the shopmen and the astuteness of the buyer. Business seemed rather dull, and the air of languor did not promise great things for the Damascene merchants. We were taken, for a little variety, into a grand courtyard which was the establishment of a great merchant. The solemn arches were standing gloomy, around were piles of stuff of one kind and another, while we who really only came to see were taken up to the second floor, where in a little room in one corner was seated a small Arab, who asked us exorbitant prices for some silk things which we did not want and did not take. I strayed from him out into the gallery which ran around the court, giving access to the various rooms, and surveyed the great stacks of goods of divers kinds, and wondered how a house, dealing in such valuable goods and in large amounts, could ever condescend to haggle over a silk handkerchief. But this is the tendency of the East. They see no difference between a small amount and a large amount when there is something to be made.

When my companions had found out that the gentleman within would not sell at a reasonable figure they came out, and we went to see the Great Mosque, which opens directly from the bazaars. We passed through the covered way, for most of the streets which are lined with shops have a roof over them, directly to the entrance of the mosque, which was formerly an old Christian church. The original gateway remains, as the chalice and paten on the bronze doors testify. Above the shops is to be seen portions of the arch and pediment still remaining. An inscription in Greek runs along the top, which seems singularly out

of place, as the church has been turned from its original purposes. It reads as follows: " Thy kingdom, O Christ, is an everlasting kingdom, and thy dominion endureth throughout all generations." Perhaps the Moslems have let it remain as an evidence of its untruthfulness, in their minds. Just within the gateway is a large courtyard, with a colonnade running around three sides of it. By turning to the right we entered the mosque itself, which is four hundred and fifty feet long and one hundred and eighty broad. It is divided into three aisles and is very imposing, although there is little about it beyond its architecture and size to recommend it. The ornamentation is dingy and uninteresting, and the general aspect bare. On one side is a small sanctuary with a dome, which is supposed to cover the cave in which is preserved the head of John the Baptist, inclosed in a casket of gold. In the center of the building, resting on four massive pillars, is a dome, which is one hundred feet across and one hundred and twenty feet high. The marble floor is almost entirely covered with carpets, some of which are extremely beautiful, while others are almost entirely worn out. To walk the whole length of the building and return constitutes the necessary sight-seeing. The thought that this is a very sacred place of worship accompanies one, but it is a hard matter to understand why this place is to remain forty years after the rest of the world is destroyed, so that the faithful may pray in it. If the world is demolished, what is the use for further prayer? They say, too, that one prayer said here is worth thirty thousand said elsewhere. Surely, it amounts almost to a temptation!

We climbed the stairs of a minaret to see the view, going through stuffy, narrow passages, in which the air was close and the heat stifling. But we were rewarded by looking out upon the city which lay below us. The view was uninterrupted in every direction. The flat-roofed houses, the green suburbs, the more distant mountains, and the long stretch of the plain toward the east, all made up a very interesting, if not charming, picture. There was not much beauty,

I am free to confess. After we had gazed long enough in every direction, extent being about the only attraction, we descended and returned to the hotel.

The streets lying between were perhaps those most frequented. Crowds of people seemed to fill them as we edged our way through, seeking the horse market where we should have more space. Cafés were lighted up, shops selling sweetmeats were doing a thriving business, and just at hand a fine bath establishment offered luxurious bathing. But as it was getting late we returned to the hotel because we were feeling the pangs of hunger.

In the evening we were treated to a visit from the merchants, who came with their swords, pistols, embroidery and silk goods, to sell them to the un-wary traveler. They did not sell anything, and departed with a poor idea of us, I fancy. Mr. C——, Hilton and Leighton, lounged on the divans carrying on a desultory chat. Soon the Philologist entered accompanied by the resident missionary to the Jews. He was himself a converted Jew, and acted in the capacity of chaplain to the Consulate. At any rate he preached in the chapel which had been fitted up in one of the rooms of that place, and his mission to the hotel was to get me to preach. I declined, but he insisted with such urgency that at one time I almost yielded. However, I managed to maintain my rigid exterior, and after awhile he became convinced of my determination not to preach. Then heaving a sigh he said :

"Well, I suppose I must go and write a sermon then." I was both amused and disgusted. It was already late, near ten o'clock, and I was anxious to learn what he would produce the next morning.

The whole party went to church attended by Leighton, who did condescend this time to accompany us. In our walk we passed the spot where some time before an English missionary had been killed by some fanatical Moslems. The Pasha, who had the terrible experience of 1860 in his mind, sent down the soldiers to hang one hundred men, all to be taken from that quarter irrespective of their guilt. The awful sentence was faithfully carried out, and one hundred Moslems paid the penalty, in all probability of some one else's crime. To us it seems barbarous, but in reality it was the only thing to prevent another wholesale slaughter of the Christians, such as had previously occurred.

The awfulness of that massacre cannot be well described. The dissensions between the Moslems and the Christians had been growing greater, until at last, on the ninth of July, 1860, the whole Christian quarter was in flames. The water supplies were cut off, and the miserable creatures were hemmed in between the fire and the arms of their enemies. Colonel Churchill has so graphically described it that I must quote a bit of his description. " No sooner had Abd-el-Kader gained intelligence of the frightful disaster, than he sent his faithful Algerines into the Christian quarter, with orders to rescue all the wretched sufferers they could meet. Hundreds were safely escorted to his house before dark. Many rushed to the British Consulate. As night advanced, fresh hordes of marauders, Kurds, Arabs, Druses, entered the city and swelled the furious mob of fanatics, who now, glutted with spoil, began to cry for blood. The dreadful work then began. All through that awful night, and the whole of the following day, the pitiless massacre went on. To attempt to detail all the atrocities which were committed, would be repugnant to the feelings, and useless. Hundreds disappeared, hurried away to distant parts of the surrounding country, where they were instantly married to Mohamedans. Men of all ages, from the boy to the old man, were forced to apostatize, were circumcised on the spot in derision, and then put to death. The churches and convents, which in the first paroxysm of terror had been filled to suffocation, presented piles of corpses, mixed up promiscuously with the wounded, and those only half dead, whose last agonies were endured amidst flaming beams and calcined blocks of stone falling upon them with earthquake shock. The thoroughfares were choked with the slain. To say that the Turks took no means whatever to stay this huge deluge of massacre and fire would be superfluous. They connived at it ; they instigated it ; they ordered it ; they shared in it. Abd-el-Kader alone stood between the living and the dead. Fast as his Algerines brought in those whom he had rescued, he reassured them, consoled them, fed them. He had himself gone out and brought in numbers personally. Forming them into detached parties he forwarded them under successive guards to the castle. There, as the terrific day closed in, nearly twelve thousand of all ages and sexes were collected and huddled together, a fortunate but exhausted retinue, fruits of his untiring exertions. There they remained for weeks lying on the bare ground without covering, hardly with clothing, exposed to the sun's scorching rays. Their rations scantily served out ; cucumbers and coarse bread. Lest they might obtain an unreserved repose, the Turkish soldiers kept alarming them with rumors of an approaching irruption, when they would all be given to the sword.

"Abd-el-Kader himself was now menaced. His house was filled with fugitives, European consuls and native Christians. The Mohammedans, furious at being thus baulked of their prey, advanced toward it, declaring they would have them. Informed of the movement, the hero coolly ordered his horse to be saddled, put on his cuirass and helmet, and mounting drew his sword. His faithful followers formed around him, brave remnant of his old guard, comrades in many a well-fought field, illustrious victors of the Moulaia, where, on the 18th of December, 1847, 2,500 men under his inspiring command attacked the army of the Emperor of Morocco, 60,000 strong, and entirely defeated it. The fanatics came in sight. Singly he charged into their midst and drew up. 'Wretches!' he ex-

claimed, 'is this the way you honor the Prophet? May his curses be upon you! Shame upon you, shame! You will yet live to repent. You think you may do as you please with the Christians, but the day of retribution will come. The Franks will yet turn your mosques into churches. Not a Christian will I give up. They are my brothers. Stand back or I will give my men the order to fire.' The crowd dispersed. Not a man of that Moslem throng dared raise his voice or lift his arm against the renowned champion of Israel."

The French and English interfered, and by their promptness saved the whole Christian population in Syria from destruction. The Moslems imagined that the Sultan had issued a decree for the extermination of all Christians. As a result the governor of Damascus was shot. Three Turkish officers shared the same fate, and one hundred and seventeen individuals with them. Four hundred of the lower orders were condemned to prison and exile, and fifty-six citizens hanged. Eleven of the notables were sent to Rhodes, where they lived in comfort. This was the only punishment by which the loss of 2,000,000 pounds of property and six thousand lives was avenged. The conduct of Abd-el-Kader is in itself heroic, and relieves these cruel people from entire ignominy. To-day there is quiet, peaceful calm, and nothing at all to indicate that within a few years such violent rage had seized the people. The Arab spirit has been crushed by repeated disasters, and, probably, such a frightful state of things will not occur again. The French nation built the diligence road, the only respectable thoroughfare in all this country, so that now there is a rapid means of communication from the sea to the interior.

We found the house of the British consul, which was a beautiful specimen of Damascene dwelling, with a court, fountain, and lewan. The chapel was small but comfortable, and thoroughly English in its appointments. The chaplain preached, as might be expected, a very ordinary sermon. I learned afterward in Beirût that he had been whipped by the Turkish authorities for trying to bring goods into the city without paying the custom's duties. The story seems quite probable, although I regretted to hear it, because he would thus stand in so ridiculous a light as to paralyze all Christian work in that region.

The most attractive parts of Damascus are the suburbs, which extend on the western side both north and south. The road leading to Banias we had traversed, and had received a first taste of the city from the luxuriant gardens through which it ran. Truly Damascus seems a paradise when one saunters through these attractive places on a bright, sunny day, when the sun, not too hot, gives an excuse for shade. What matters it then if the ground is dried mud and the water has a little of the golden hue? There are pleasant paths in every direction; shrubbery, trees, houses almost hidden behind the leafy screen. Then there is a mystery, a certain feeling, that this is no common place, but the very home of the Arabian Nights. I am sure we felt impressed this way, or we should never have spent the entire Sunday afternoon in wandering about these places. We took the dragoman for a walk, not Leighton, but one whom he in his grandeur hired to show us around. If he suggested that we go in one direction to see something, we immediately informed him that we were going in the other. He had nothing to do but submit. Within the walls the city is closely built, but without all is freshness, or "dampness," as Mr. Warner would say.

One ofttimes dreams that an oasis is a most delightful spot, not because it is more lovely in itself than other places, but because around it is the dreary desert. Thus it is with Damascus. It is an oasis, because far out into the plain there is nothing but sterile soil, no water, but utter desolation, like that we saw when we came over the ridge of Hermon. So wherever the two rivers send their refreshing water there is vegetation and delight, but beyond, nothing. It seems as though this was the Garden of Eden, shut off from the outside world by the desert which lies around it. Indeed, the Prophet is said to have stood hard by the heights of Salahiyeh, and after gazing at the city below, said, as he turned away : " Man can have but one Paradise, and my Paradise is fixed above."

Perhaps some of the great attractions of the suburbs are the cafés, which abound on all sides. Men sit there chatting, happy and jovial, as they would in Paris, but in different costume and with a different language. Surely the Syrians are a pleasure-loving people, and among themselves seem united and independent. In fact, nothing can surpass the fine appearance a true Syrian gentleman presents when in his refined and striking costume.

Into one of the cafés we turned our dragoman and made him order something. We did not, of course, know what we wanted, and after it came we discovered that we did not want it. So we left the dragoman to finish it and explored the garden. Little tables set around, chairs, arbors, vines, running water, across which were thrown bridges, and quaint little houses made up a very interesting tout-ensemble. All that afternoon we led the life of a Damascene, taking a rest from the toils of our late journey, and refreshing ourselves for the next, which, I must say, we dreaded.

There is so little to describe in Damascus, but so much to interest and delight one, that it can only be a sort of dream, which is sternly unreal unless there be in the mind a fancy for such things. To the ordinary sightseer who comes only to carry away data, there is, perhaps, not much. Thus I find so few care to linger long in this spot, of which we first hear when we read the story of Abraham. His steward was from Damascus, and probably was proud of the fact. Then we read of the Hadads, who were such uncomfortable neighbors of Israel. Then the story of Naaman, when he cast such a dreadful imputation on the river Jordan. After this dynasty had failed, the city came into the hand of Tiglath-pileser, king of Assyria. For a thousand years it was held captive, although in commerce it was still great. When the kingdom of the Seleucidae was divided, Cyzicenus fixed his residence in the city. The next great event was when it surrendered to Pompey in B. C. 64. In 634 A. D., it fell into the hands of the Moslems. Soon after its capture the Khalif made it the seat of his government, and the glory of his empire spread in a manner almost suggestive of witchcraft. So the old city became the capital of an empire reaching from the Himalayas to the Atlantic. Great pains were taken to render Damascus beautiful; the Great Mosque was built, and the Arab historians delight to expatiate upon its gorgeousness. From this time decay set in, and only the reigns of Nureddin and his more distinguished successor, Saladin, form bright epochs in the city's history. Two centuries later came Tamerlane, "the wild beast," who laid the city in ashes, pillaged its palaces, its houses, and its libraries. An indiscriminate massacre followed, and the horrors of that day still come down by tradition to the present century. Later the Turks gained possession of it, and retain their hold, but it is fast slipping away.

Thus we have a range of history of the greatest possible variety and interest. Surely if Damascus was not a paradise there is enough to cause the scholar to stop and reflect. In the reign of the Khalifs what glory and beauty must have covered all this ground! What learning, what store of wealth, what grandeur!

We had one more day in this delightful city, and
I am sure we all dreaded the thought of moving on.
The Philologist and his wife decided to go to
Beirût by diligence, and their parting request of
the dragoman was that I should have the horse the
lady rode through the country.   I was pleased with
the prospect, and thanked them effusively.   Leighton said it should be so.   Monday morning we all

went to see some native houses.   The two which we
entered have been described so many times, that

it seems almost useless to do so again. But for the benefit of a few, I will say they were both around courts. The interior aspect was beautiful, the exterior bare and common. Striped lines of marble, after the Damascus fashion, decorated the court. The reception-hall of the first into which we were shown was a beautiful specimen of inlaid marble, but done in imitation of Western ideas, and not at all consistent with the beautiful patterns of the East. The room was lofty, large, and costly to a wonderful degree, but it lacked the Eastern flavor. European chairs stood about, giving the whole a grotesque appearance. In short, it seemed to be the whim of a man who had no ideas of beauty, but reckoned it only by its cost. The other house was more distinctly Oriental. The courtyard was large and pleasant. The reception-room occupied one side, being of vast extent. The walls were lined with divans, and a fountain was supposed to play in the center. It looked dreary and deserted. Little light came into the windows, and the advent of the daughter of the house, dressed in a common flannel petticoat, with a black silk sack and French slippers, dispelled whatever illusion we might otherwise have had. Besides, she was decidedly unkempt, and not at all clean, so that when we were introduced and were stared at, we began to feel uneasy and withdrew. A Damascene house might be a paradise, but in reality it is in most cases a miserable dwelling.

After dinner Leighton came up the stairs of the hotel, looking very mysterious, and said he had something to show me. I could hardly understand his manner, but followed him to the street, where he pointed out a nice-looking horse. I gazed at it stupidly enough, and he looked at me questioningly.

"Well," said I, "what of it?"

"This is a horse I want you to try."

"When?"

"This afternoon."

"What for?"

"To ride the rest of the journey."

"But I am going to have Mrs. ——'s horse."

"Yes, I know you are, but just try this and see how you like it."

"Very well," I replied, "I will do so," and then returned to the divan in the hotel where Hilton and myself were having a chat.   At last the young men of the party gathered themselves together for a ride about the walls. We were introduced to a German, who did not speak English, but was to escort us. If I had not been familiar with his native tongue we should have had a doleful excursion. As it was he took us around the walls to the place where they say St. Paul was let down in a basket. The walls are now in a state of decay, being made of mud dried into bricks, thus easily disintegrating from the action of the sun and the weather. The aspect of desolation on this side of the city is very great. On both sides are cemeteries, and the bones of animals, or perhaps human beings, are exposed. All the carelessness of the Orient appears, and the crumbling gate of Shurky adds to the general desolation. Our

ride was not so pleasant as our walk had been the day before, and my horse, which Leighton thought to be such a fine animal, made my ride anything but comfortable. He had a breakneck pace which threatened every moment to precipitate both him and me into the dust. When I returned to the hotel Leighton was waiting outside.

"I shall never ride that animal," I exclaimed.

"Why not?" he asked, apparently very much hurt because I could not admire him.

"He rides like an earthquake," was my only response. "Don't fail to see that Mrs. ——'s horse is ready for me in the morning." Saying this I disappeared into the hotel.

XIX.

Lebanon.

TUESDAY morning with heavy hearts we began our preparations for another week of tenting. There is nothing so extremely stupid as romance when one has become sated with it. Tents and horseback-riding soon weary one, and the prospect of four days in the saddle and four more nights in the tents was decidedly depressing. Thus we were gloomy enough, and not a few envied the Philologist, who having seen Baalbek could mount the diligence like a civilized being and ride into Beirût. I strolled down the stairs, having bidden farewell to the cool, beautiful room in the hotel Victoria, and wearily asked for my horse. A small crowd of Arabs, among whom were some of our servants, stood around the doorway, and the horse I had ridden the day before was brought up.

"That is not my horse," I remarked calmly.

"But it is," persisted some one, while Leighton tried to get out of my sight. I called to him and demanded what this meant.

"Ask the muleteer," he said laconically.

"I can do that very easily," I said sarcastically. "Where is Mrs. ——'s horse, which I was to have?"

"The muleteer says he is sick."

"I don't believe it," I replied, "I never saw such trickery. Let me . see the horse. I can tell whether he is sick or not." Leighton looked crushed, but turned to the muleteer, who had a look of terrible perplexity. A rapid and voluble conversation took place in Arabic and I stood by, looking as angry as I knew how.

"The horse is very sick," Leighton said, trying to be concerned, although the scamp knew all the time that it was only a ruse of the muleteer. At last I attacked him in good forcible English, which, as it is rather a harsh language, made some impression, I trust. Then it came out that the horse had been sent out of town and was not available. I tried to give the rascal, both rascals in fact, an idea that I was going to injure some one ; outwardly they seemed to feel the danger, but inwardly I am convinced they laughed. Finally Leighton said :

"I don't see what you can do better than ride this horse."

"I will walk first," I cried. I then threatened to

write up Cook, Leighton, the muleteer, and every one that I knew, in the London *Times*, not that I had the least idea it would do any good, but because I have always heard Englishmen use this as the last most terrible threat. I acknowledged to myself, in spite of my anger, that I would soon forget all about it, like the rest of the poor abused people who have reason to dislike Cook. The sympathetic remarks of my companions, however, did not tend to soothe me.

"What are you going to do?" asked Leighton after a while, with incomparable impudence.

"Ride my old horse, of course," I replied. "If he dies, all right. I hope he may. To cause Cook or this scoundrel expense," I said, indicating the perplexed muleteer by a wave of my hand, "would cause me delight." The dilapidated old horse was brought up and I mounted him. The first thing I did was to borrow Leighton's spurs. Armed with them and my riding-whip I trusted to finish the journey without great difficulty.

At last we started, and left the city by the Salahiyeh road. I cannot say I was especially delighted with the scenery. I had not yet recovered from my anger, and was too intent upon keeping out of Leighton's way, fearing I should be likely to say something not befitting my dignity. As we rode up the heights, which are the first outshoots of the Lebanon range, we paused near a wely to view the city which we had just left.   A harder-hearted man than myself would have yielded to the influence of the beauty which was spread out before us.   From the crest of the hill the

plain stretched out far toward the horizon, until it was lost in the mist of the distance.   Below us was a sea of green, softly tinged with yellow from the early spring foliage, while white houses showed their tops above the trees.   Here and there rose minarets and towers, ivory white in the sun.   It was a wilderness of bloom, olive, apricot, plum, and walnut vying with each other, while roses and jasmin, babbling brooks and rivulets abounded.   Close up to this forest of ver-dure came the yellow desert.   Behind us rose the bleak sides of Lebanon, into whose recesses we were soon to plunge. As we turned away we saw dark clouds coming with great rapidity over the mountains. It looked seriously like rain, and, turning to Leighton, I suggested as much. But he laughed at the idea; said, in fact, that the signs were altogether against it. I was crushed and said no more, until riding down the side of the elevation I felt a few drops of rain. Then I insisted that we should try to catch up with the baggage train, and get our thick coats and waterproofs. But he still persisted in his belief that it was only a cloud, which would soon blow over. So I could only grumble to myself.

"If I get wet," I said at last, "you will be responsible."

"You can have my mackintosh."

"All right," I replied, "I shall have it then, and if you get wet, you may blame yourself."

We rode on, the wind increasing but the sun shining, through bare, chalk hills to the flinty plain of Sahra. After riding about an hour we came to a glen, down which we turned to the left, amid terraced vineyards and orchards, where we were so protected from the wind that we did not feel its violence as when unsheltered by the hills. The scenery became wilder as we descended, and the valley of the Barada, or the Abana, as the ancients called it, appeared before us. At the narrowest part the torrent left scarcely a foot-path, and in the rocks overhead is a tunnel, which, probably, once conveyed the waters of the fountain of Fijeh to Damascus. The gorge which we entered was extremely beautiful, and after passing some houses we came to the fountain itself, with its wonderful flow of waters. Trees were standing thickly around, 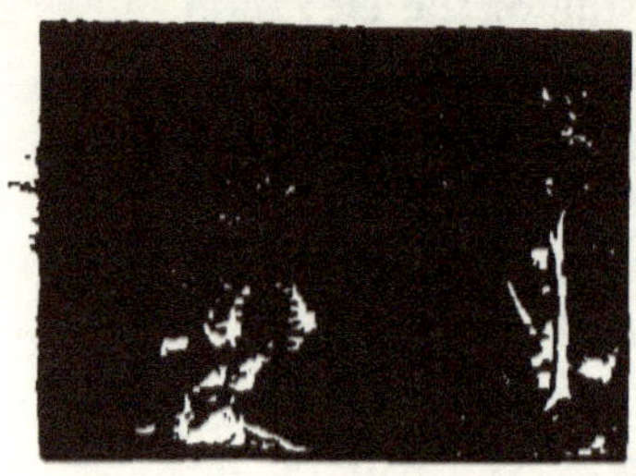 groves and orchards lined the river, while walnut, poplar, apricot, apple, and cherry formed a dense underwood. The hamlet near by consisted of about thirty houses. The fountain bursts from a narrow cave under an old temple at the base of a shelving cliff. Just over the fountain is a platform of masonry, and down in the stream a great mass of stones have fallen. To the right of the fountain are the ruins of a building about thirty feet square.

The scene is extremely picturesque, set, as it is, in the very heart of the mountains of Anti-Lebanon, and, had the day not promised rain so liberally, we should have been in a position to enjoy ourselves. We had decided to take our luncheon here, but the drops of rain falling fast decided us to seek shelter in one of the neighboring houses. A servant was dispatched to seek a place, and soon returning took us to the principal house, that belonging to the head man. Within it was much cleaner than we expected, and, although we did not disturb the family by entering the house proper, we could see from our position under a kind of portico what the establishment was like. Soon we were cheered by the sun which came out after it had rained but little, and in spite of our forebodings about the weather were a merry party. Our quarters were of necessity somewhat contracted, but the novelty of eating in a native house, which had been, I fancy, swept clean for our reception, entirely nullified this difficulty. The remnants of the luncheon were given to the family, and they, doubtless, thought us princes, since probably they had never before tasted food so fine.

The house was made of mud, thickly plastered upon poles. The roofs were a kind of thatch, also covered with mud. The whole establishment was a series of huts, low, cramped, and, I fancy, uncomfortable. We gave our hospitable hosts a buksheesh and continued our journey. Leaving this wild spot we wound up the glen, and soon found that it widened into a valley, in which were orchards, while the hills were covered with terraces. Thus we came at last to Suk. Beyond this place we again entered a narrow glen and soon crossed a bridge of a single arch. The parapets having fallen, the undertaking seemed at first hazardous. But the horses did not shy or hesitate and soon we were over. We paused awhile at the other side, for the wind was still blowing a gale.

The scene was truly grand, and such was the impression I had of the Lebanons, that I wish greatly at some future time to ride through them again, when the cold is less piercing and the wind less severe. The stream below us tumbled over rocks and stones making a sound which drove away the awful stillness, which otherwise would have reigned supreme. The mountains seemed piled one on the other, rising up to what seemed enormous heights. Indeed the ride might have been sublime and even the misery of our hands, cut by the hail and blue with cold, could not entirely deprive us of admiration. When we started Leighton sent the party on ahead, but soon came up lashing his horse in a cruel manner. We did not suspect the cause then, so when he asked me for one of his spurs I foolishly gave it to him. We had now entered the glen of the Barada. The cliffs were several hundred feet high, and the mountains rose over them a thousand feet more. Here Leighton acted in a manner to alarm the whole party. It soon became evident that he had taken too much liquor. Now he would ride his horse in a furious manner past us, and then pull him up until we expected to see both horse and rider go over the precipice. The white coat of the horse began to be stained with blood, and soon his whole side was bleeding from the furious way in which Leighton used the spur. Expostulation seemed to do no good. At times Leighton would leave the party for a half hour. Had we not another dragoman we should have been in great danger, and been far more alarmed than we were.

At last we emerged from the glen, and came into the upland plain of Zebdani. The beauty of the scene was so marred by the storm and our composure so disturbed by the conduct of our dragoman, that we had only one thought, to reach our tents. But now that we had left the shelter of the mountains, we experienced the full fury of the blast. A perfect hurricane came over Jebel-esh-Sharki blowing snow and hail directly into our faces, until it seemed at times almost impossible to endure it longer. So great was the pain inflicted by the wind and hail, that at times I looked to see if my hands were not really cut. The horse almost refused to move forward, and the sleet was so thick that the members of the party could hardly keep in sight of each other. My poor old horse at one time stopped short, and being as usual behind, gave me

the uncomfortable sensation of being deserted. No
shelter was nearer than our tents, several miles off.
Leighton had entirely disappeared, being far ahead.
We continued thus for two hours, and by the time
the storm had begun to diminish in force we saw
the camping-ground before us, and were soon able
to dismount. Seizing our luggage and putting on
our coats, we gathered around the cook's fire to get
a little warmth. We awaited dinner with great
anxiety, and, as soon as we could conveniently,
sought our beds, where we managed with great difficulty to keep warm through the night. I put my
clothes on my bed, and over all my great rubber
coat, so I did not actually suffer.

In the morning we awoke to ice and snow. Our
basins were frozen over, and the landscape was entirely white. But we felt more cheerful, for the sun
was shining and we were one day nearer Beirût.
At any rate it was only one more day's ride to Baalbek, and there, surely, we would be better off. The
Plain of Zebdani is in the center of the Anti-Lebanon Range. It is about eight miles long and two
wide. As we looked down toward the south we
saw Jebel-esh-Sheikh, or Mount Hermon, which we
had seen now from nearly every side, standing
with its snow-white covering against a light gray
sky. The mountains to the west rose up six thousand feet above the sea, while those to the east
were even higher but not quite so bold. Winter

seemed to spread its snowy mantle over the whole
scene.

To eat our breakfast and remount was not so irk-
some as it would have been did we not feel that by
so doing we were approaching something better.
By the time we started, although it was still very
chilly, the sun had already melted the snow. We
were of course protected by our great-coats and
rubber coverings, and all that morning we splashed
through the mud and water. We crossed another
mountain and found ourselves on the Plain of Surg-
haya. We discovered, after much looking, a spot
which was protected from the wind, and dry, where
we could have our luncheon. Under a rock which
gave us shelter, we formed, in spite of our reverses,
a merry party. We were beginning to get over the
annoyance which we had felt before, and had in fact
forgiven Leighton, who was the most penitent of
men. He said he had to take whisky because he
got wet from having loaned his water-proof coat.
My mouth was closed, although I did remark that
I had suggested rain when we left Damascus. But
we were happier, and could find it possible to tease
the widow who bore our bantering surprisingly well.
The rest of the journey was over more mountains,
till we descended into the lovely Plain of Buka'a,
which lies between Lebanon and Anti-Lebanon.
As we came to the top of the ridge and could look
both south and north and see the great sweep of

country, which was so wonderfully walled in between these two great ranges, it required only warmer and pleasanter weather to send us into raptures. As it was I think we all took it calmly, although candor must compel one to admit that it was very beautiful. Below us toward the north lay Baalbek. Hither we directed our way, and I used on poor old Bucephalus all my energies. We were in no mood for ecstasy, we simply wanted shelter and a fire.

XX.

Baalbek.

WE rode into Baalbek like a party of adventurers uncertain what reception awaited them. We knew the place afforded a hotel, and I do not mind confessing we expected to be sheltered within its comfortable walls. We said as much to Leighton, but he demurred, and replied, in fact, that the hotel was not good, a statement which I have seen contradicted. We then began to meditate, but were met by the camp-servants, who had come on ahead, and told us that the governor, or whatever official he was, had forbidden us access to the ruins. The tents were not up. We had ridden all day, and were cold. Here was a pretty state of things, and with one accord we turned to Leighton to help us out. We insisted upon being entertained at Mr.

Cook's expense at the hotel. It was useless. Leighton had orders never to go to a hotel unless it rained. Poor fellow, why was he not as scrupulous about whisky?

At last he relented to the extent of permitting us to go, until the tents were put up, to the other hotel, which is the only means I have of describing what was known as the rival establishment of the Victoria, from whose landlord we hardly escaped with our lives, so persistent was he. Here we were put into a good-sized room, furnished with a divan and some chairs. We ordered tea on our own responsibility, and for an hour were happy. It is astonishing how attached one can become to a place when obliged to leave it for another affording less comfort. The hotel was simply a native house, which had been cleaned and turned into a rival establishment. An English lady, who had married a foreigner with a title, was stopping there, and seemed to like it well enough to remain. This spoke well for the proprietor. But Leighton was pitiless, and made us all return to the camp, where the ladies, after a little experience of the cold, determined not to stay. So they went back to the hotel and passed the night, intending to take the diligence back to Beirût in the morning.

Another night was spent in the chilly tents; the romance had entirely fled, and even the most enthusiastic one of the party, Mr. W——, had nothing to say. We all strongly advocated seeing the ruins hastily the next morning, and then to go on to Beirût, but Leighton said "no." The caravan was ordered, from London, I suppose, to move at just such a pace, and it could go no faster. We were due in Beirût Saturday night, and not one moment sooner should we get there. Thus we were compelled, against our wishes, to see more of the ruins than we intended. After it was all over, we did not care so much, for the day passed more pleasantly than we had expected.

Baalbek is of world-wide celebrity, its ruins being at once impressive from their grandeur, and interesting from the haze in which their origin is shrouded. As grand as they are, it seems strange that we have no exact account of them, but are left to guess from side-lights how these great temples were erected. It is almost impossible to give a full and accurate description of them. They are so stupendous, so much larger in reality than one fancies at a distance from them, that he hesitates to attempt the recital of their glories.

These temples formed an acropolis, like the one at Athens. A broad flight of steps, one hundred and fifty feet wide, led up from the city, which, we may easily imagine, lay all around, to a grand portico with twelve massive pillars. On either side was a tower, which contained a room thirty-five feet square. The walls were nearly twenty feet thick.

22

Everything was on so grand a scale that the mind refuses almost to comprehend the vastness. The entrance is now built up, because the Turks used the ruins for a fortress. But from within we saw the octagonal court lined with columns. A triple gateway led from the portico into this, which was in the

shape of a hexagon, two hundred feet across. Beyond this was the great court, four hundred by four hundred and fifty feet. At regular spaces were niches elaborately carved and joined by rows of columns. Originally this court was free from buildings, but a Christian basilica was erected here, and the ruins of it are scattered all around. The great temple, now a mass of ruins, stood directly opposite the entrance, a glorious structure, if the six columns still standing can give us any idea of its magnitude. They are about sixty feet in height, bordered with a frieze. The temple itself was three hundred feet long and two hundred and forty feet broad. In all there were fifty-four columns, measuring, at least, seven feet in diameter. The whole height of the building must have been over ninety feet. Blocks of stone are scattered all around, but there are no remains of the walls of the temple, so it is thought that it was never completed, but was merely an open space consecrated to the worship of the sun.

The whole of this magnificent structure stood upon massive walls nearly fifty feet high, and, rising thus one hundred and forty feet above the surrounding plain, was, doubtless, very imposing. In these walls are the great stones which have caused so much wonder to engineers. One is sixty-four feet long, thirteen feet thick, and about thirteen feet wide. Two others are very nearly as large, and nine other stones are thirty feet long and thirteen feet in their other proportions. How these enormous blocks were brought for a mile and put in place, twenty feet above the ground, must remain a mystery. Examination shows that the sub-structure was of a much earlier date than the temples themselves, which, so far as can be ascertained, were erected about one hundred and fifty years after our Lord's birth.

One never tires of looking at the six great columns which tower up above everything else in this mass of ruins. Even the

Temple of Jupiter, which stands just beside them, cannot keep the attention entirely away from these grand remnants of a brilliant undertaking. While the latter temple is small when compared to the other, it is still the largest temple standing in Syria, and for decoration and design surpasses anything except the Pantheon at Athens. It is two hundred and seventeen feet by one hundred and seventeen. The style is Corinthian, and its sculptured ornaments show that it is coeval, or nearly so, with the great temple. In all there were fifty columns around the walls. Now many of them have fallen, and perhaps the temple is far more picturesque as it is than it was formerly. Some views of it, one especially where the column is leaning against the wall, is extremely attractive. The height of these columns is sixty-five feet, and their diameter about six feet. The portal is twenty-one feet wide and forty-two feet high. All around it is ornamented most profusely. The central piece of stone has dropped somewhat and is now supported by a clumsy pier of stone, built by the Turks to keep it from falling.

The same luxuriance of ornamentation exists within. All about the temple is evidence of the most beautiful design; and although critics may find fault with its decoration, as not being pure, it is still very fascinating, and withal so grand as to hold the attention if it is in a false style. One sits down on the ruins to try to comprehend the greatness of the place. Such desolation reigns everywhere that only a tinge of sadness remains after long contemplation. Not long since these beautiful specimens of heathen art stood almost entire, but the iconoclastic hand of the Arab, or the Turk, has destroyed so much, that to-day we wonder at what we see, and regret that which we might have seen had the possessors of this land been less bigoted.

Going down through the vaults to the gateway we mounted our horses and rode out into the country, passing the beautiful little Temple of Venus, which

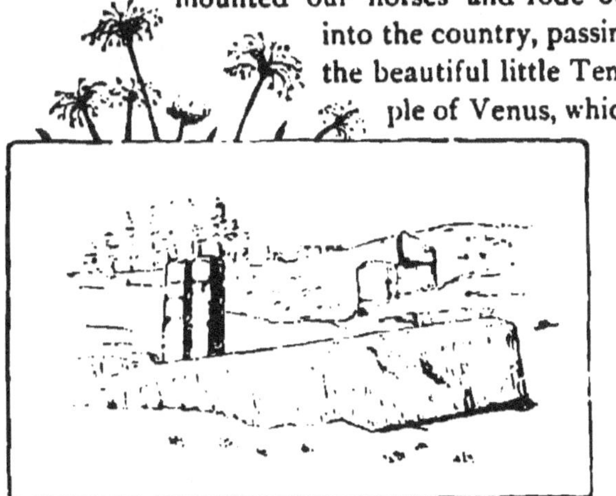

stands, without the acropolis, by itself in the fields. It is a circular structure with six columns. Thence

we rode through the town to the quarries where
there still remains the great stone, larger than any
in the wall, already hewn but never moved. It is
sixty-eight feet long, fourteen feet wide, and nearly
the same in breadth. It weighs more than eleven
hundred tons. The view of the ruins from the
quarries is very picturesque. Over a sea of pur-
plish almond trees, which are budding into bloom,

rises the wall of the fortress. This is surmounted
by the six graceful columns, which with their reddish tint contrast beautifully with the little foliage
around.   If one has not examined the ruins carefully and judged well of their extent, he will hardly
imagine they are so great, when viewing them from
a distance.

When Baalbek was first founded we have no
knowledge. The colossal platform on which the
temples were erected is doubtless coeval with
Phœnician prosperity. We conclude that it was a
holy place of that remarkable people. Julius Cæsar

made the place, then known as Heliopolis, a Roman colony. In the second century it was celebrated for its oracle, so that the Emperor Trajan consulted it previously to his second expedition against the Parthians. It seems astonishing that no contemporary historian refers to the erection of the temples, but the first mention of them is found in a writer of the seventh century. From him we learn that Antoninus Pius built, at Heliopolis of Phœnician Lebanon, a great temple to Jupiter, which was one of the wonders of the world.

When the Moslems captured the place in the seventh century, they changed the name back to Baalbek, and converted it into a fortress. Since that time it has gradually declined in importance, and instead of a great and flourishing city, it is now a small village, the center of a Turkish garrison which keeps the district of Lebanon in order.

Hilton and myself rode out in the afternoon because we found the time hang heavily upon our hands. We had implored Leighton to move on, for we were certain to reach Zahleh by sundown, but he would not agree to our wishes. The day grew warmer, so that after all we had no great difficulty in enjoying ourselves. It was delightful to feel perfectly free and independent in a strange country. Hitherto we had been so bound down by the dragoman that we hardly dared have him out of our sight. But in this great plain there was not the

least danger of being lost.   Mrs. W—— had directed
that I should have her horse for the rest of the
journey, and I signified to Leighton that if I were
deprived of it there would be a little discomfort for
him when I reached civilization.   Mr. C—— and
the Presbyterian minister got on much better after
the widow departed, and I am not sure but Mr.
C—— would have abandoned his ritualistic proclivities and changed his faith, had the journey continued a little longer.

The next morning we left the camp and Baalbek,
setting our faces steadfastly toward Beirût.   The

sun rose bright and pleas-
ant and there was nothing
but the memory of our
chilly experience in the
mountains of Anti-Leb-
anon to cause us discom-
fort.   The road was excellent, as good as it could
possibly be without some
kind of pavement.   The
way passes by the quarries down into the valley,
with green fields beside it, and the distant top of
Hermon in front.   Soon we crossed the stream
which rises at Baalbek and forms later on in its
course the Litany.   An occasional village, with its
low houses made of stone and plastered with mud,
diverted the attention.   We passed the ruins of a

massive temple, but did not stop to investigate them ; then the village which contains the reputed tomb of Noah. The tomb measures seventy yards in length and is covered by a low building. Within were votive offerings and cloth coverings. One could not but reflect that Noah must have been a very large man to need so much space in which to be buried. Some one suggests that it was probably an old aqueduct, which somehow seems a little disrespectful.

So we continued until about noon, when we reached Zahleh, the largest village in Lebanon. The street through which we passed appeared prosperous, and like that of a city. Houses stood up on the hills around, and from the opposite side of the river we could get a good idea of its extent. Vineyards and terraces surround the town, and the bare hills rise above it. While not especially at-

tractive, it is still not disagreeable, and has not so great an amount of filth as one generally sees. The American missionary resident here had been a classmate of the Presbyterian, and under the guidance of Mr. C——'s dragoman, he hunted him up. We crossed the stream meanwhile, and took up our station on the bank opposite the town, where we attracted many curious idlers of the place, who evidently thought it a privilege to see us eat. Soon the missionary rode up with our friend, and we all had an opportunity to gain a little knowledge about missions in this quarter. So far as I could learn, they consisted mostly in teaching the children of the Greek and Roman families. There was a reserve about the missionaries, for there were two present, which I could hardly understand. Was it possible that they had become discouraged, or had found the field less fertile than they expected?

From Zahleh to Shtora, the station on the French road, was a ride of about an hour and a half. We saw the shabby station-house and its miserable hotel, and were glad that we had our own clean quarters a little farther up on the main road to Beirût. While we were lounging around the camp, waiting for night to close in, we were treated to a visit from Turkish soldiers, who were encamped in the vicinity. They were a new squad that had been drafted up in the country, and were commanded by a lieutenant who had received his education in Europe, that is, as much of an education as he possessed. He came to see us, and talked amicably in wretched French, which we answered in French equally wretched. His clothes were much the worse for wear, and his rank was not so distinctly marked as to be very observable. The soldiers were raw recruits, driven almost like sheep in a herd.

The morning broke with perfectly clear sky, one of the finest days I ever saw. Hilton and myself, knowing we had nothing to miss and could not lose our way, determined to ride into Beirût at our own sweet will, and for once be free from the slow pace of the dragoman. We inquired of Leighton where we should find the hotel, which one of the two it was, and then set out. But before leaving I learned of another attempt of the muleteer to deprive me of my horse. Apparently Leighton had some fear that even my good humor would become exhausted. Thus it happened that I rode Mrs. W——'s animal and was enabled to enjoy the ride.

For a long time the road wound up among the mountains, whose rocky sides ascended high above us or fell off far below. Still the journey being on the ascent did not present any very grand features. The road was magnificent, kept in as good repair as

any city pavement and vastly better than that of
our American cities. As it was early spring, there
did not appear to be much foliage as we came near
the top of the mountain, but as we turned the last
corner and began to descend the view became finer.
We passed the troop of soldiers, led by the lieutenant with whom we had conversed the night before,
and pitied their miserable condition. Occasionally
a house or a station of the diligence company enlivened the scene, but for the most part the road

seemed deserted. But shortly we came
to the point where the country opens
up shelving toward the sea. Off in
the distance lay the exquisitely blue
water, rising high into the sky, yet
being softly dimmed as it approached
the horizon, because from where we
stood the distance seen was very great.
The configuration of the coast could be
traced for many a mile, and far out in
the distance, at a point of land, we could discern
Beirût. It is needless to say we paused to fully
comprehend what was before us. A more perfect
panorama could hardly be imagined. The softness
of the colors, cerulean blue against the yellows and
the brown of the shore, was something to drive an
artist mad. The dark spots against the sides of -
the hills broken and jagged were trees clumped
together. Deep gullies represented rivers. There

were bold masses of rock, capes, and withal a dim shining clump of white boulders as they seemed, which were the houses of the city. Winding down these vast rocks was the road, doubling itself like a serpent, but visible through nearly all its course. It seemed such a little way, but still it took several hours for us to travel it. Besides, it was so steep that it looked, from our standpoint, almost dangerous. Far to the north and far to the south the mountains fell off, and high above us were the more lofty peaks of the Lebanon Range. Surely the beauty of this district has not been exaggerated. Under the genial sunshine of spring, when not too hot, all nature seemed a paradise.

And so we slowly continued our journey, eager to reach the pearl which lay below us. Like a man who sees jewels before him we were hardly content to wait, but hastened to seize everything in one grasp. Thus through vineyards, past villages, places where the residents of Beirût spend the summer, we descended into the more fertile, and perhaps less beautiful country near the sea. But streams were murmuring all around us, trees formed artistic groups, a villa nestling among shrubbery made the whole romantic, and so, delighted, warmed, and sometimes even thrilled, we came nearer to the plain. Far below us, on our right, was a vast chasm, causing us to shudder in looking down, at the bottom of which ran the river Beirût. Aqueducts, bridges, and ofttimes mills, could be distinguished far below. Then the road at last seemed to have  reached the level, and for awhile we rode on even ground, past a huge grove, where we saw signs of life, occasional caravans, horsemen and even people in carriages; then came cactus-hedges, houses set back from the road, and very soon the streets of the city itself.

A last long gallop and we found ourselves in the great square or market-place, around which were buildings and shops. Hilton, who had been in Beirût before, fancied he knew the hotel, and so trusting entirely to luck we rode on. Soon we came to a large square building, and dismounting were happily at the right place. We were tired, and demanding a room, were shown into it at once. This was extremely fortunate for me, for tired and weary by my journey I was glad to be able to be in a decent place once more and to feel free again. Our luggage happily had just arrived, the servants were in attendance, and so I could replenish some parts of my wardrobe, which like the wonderful vehicle we read of lasted just a certain time and then gave out entirely. Had I ridden another mile I should not have been presentable in a city, and for once I judged myself lucky.

XXI.

Beirût.

To say that we were all delighted to end the trip would be to use very moderate language. While we all were thoroughly glad to accomplish and see as much as we had, not one of us would be willing to undergo the same fatigue the second time. My own impressions are that the same amount of ground could be covered with less trouble and with no greater expense. I should most strongly advise any one desiring to see the whole country, and it is well worth one's time and trouble, to enter at Jaffa quite independently. Use Cook's landaus and his other facilities, when convenient, but do not be tied down by his regulation tour. It is not more expensive, and it will insure much more pleasure and much more attention from Cook's employees. But after the money is once paid down, two hundred dollars for the thirty days' tour, there is then nothing more for them to expect. I should suggest that one remain in Jerusalem, certainly a week, perhaps two, and thence make excursions to Hebron, Bethlehem, Mar Saba, and the Jordan, returning to Jerusalem. A few days there will give the needed rest. Then take tents, or perhaps by this time there will be hotels established by the way, and go up to Nazareth. This will be a four days' ride. At Nazareth good accommodations can be had in the Convent. Thence it is an easy matter to go to the Sea of Galilee, and return by way of Mount Tabor. Then ride over from Nazareth to Haifa, in time for the steamer which touches there once a fortnight. At Beirût it is an easy matter to take the diligence to Damascus, one day's ride, or to hire a private carriage, which, while a little more expensive, is far more comfortable. Remaining in Damascus at least a week, on his return let one make a detour to Baalbek, where there is a good hotel. Thus one can see the whole country and have but four nights in the tents, something greatly to be desired. While tents are very well at first, and comfortable when the weather is pleasant, they become very wearisome after a time, and are wretched if the weather be wet, as it is quite apt to be. A delicate person runs great risks by living in them, and the monotony of the journey over Hermon and up through the Lebanon mountains is almost unendurable.

With Cook it is a matter of money. After his

party is once formed and the tents started on their northern journey, it is cheaper for him to send his parties through to Damascus. This wholesale way of traveling has made them the scoff of writers, although, in fact, excepting the arbitrary route laid out, and, perhaps, the chance of one or two disagreeable members, I am convinced that one has more real comfort than when traveling with a private dragoman. In proof of this I would cite the Hungarians, who, although very wealthy and going with their own dragoman, an accomplished Egyptian, joined our party because of the advantages offered. The sum of the whole matter is not to allow oneself to be completely under the control of Cook. When money is once paid his agents are very careless. They are pretty sure that no complaints will get back to the London office. It is always thus with mankind. They suffer indignities and imposition, and intend to make trouble, but after the annoyance has passed they determine never to expose themselves to these things again, and forget that others have to go through the same experience. One thing must be said by way of justice: I do not think the London office understands half the iniquity of its agents in the East. Indeed, it is, perhaps, remarkable how they can control their business as well as they do. While at Beirût I met a man, sent out, I fancy, for the express purpose of reporting some of the abuses.

In the circulars people are informed that there shall be no fees for the servants whatever. But I was not at all surprised to have the dragoman come around for the usual present. Most of the party weakly yielded. I am ashamed to record that I cannot remember whether I, too, encouraged this dereliction of duty or not. I think we all felt a little sympathy with the servants, for we had nothing to complain of from them. They had served us most faithfully, especially Luigi, who hung around the hotel after the rest left on the steamer for Jaffa. He said Leighton had kept the money we contributed, or, at any rate, he had not got what he should have had. Poor Luigi! Your mild eyes concealed, I fear, a wretched soul.

The most exasperating part, however, was the paper Leighton circulated, in which the signers declared their perfect approbation of his conduct and appreciation of his services. Two clergymen in good and regular standing, an eminent philologist and his wife, the widow and the high church Mr. C——, to say nothing of Hilton, who, being a very wicked young man, did not count, signed this without a murmur. The pious Mr. W—— and his really sweet and good wife demurred a little, but were overcome, because Leighton told such a pitiful tale of his utter destitution if he did not take back a good record. I fled in terror, lest my uprightness should likewise take a fall, and that valuable manuscript lacks my autograph, though, possibly, not my name.

Thus ended a month's experience, in which all classes of society may be said to have been joined. To me the mixture was excessively diverting. Had all the party been agreeable I should have suffered ennui. Mixed as they were, the good traits of some stood out so prominently that I shall always remember them with gratitude. It was an exciting chapter of my life. Could I have such varied and such unique experiences, I would take the journey again. One more episode awaited us. One of our companions, whose conduct through the whole journey had been very reprehensible, had had a tent entirely to himself. The hotel being full, it became necessary for two to share a room between them. This man seemed to fancy he had the same right to a single room that he had had to a single tent, for which he paid extra. Thus Hilton and myself, who were room-mates, were surprised to find a third bed put in our room. We suspected the cause, and summoned the servant, who explained that Dr. C——had refused to share his room with anyone, and as the obstinate American had been in our tent on the journey, therefore he could be in our room in the hotel. We declined to see the matter in the same light, and Dr. C——, who for refined selfishness ex-

ceeded anything I have yet seen, unless the widow
may be cited as an instance, was baffled. The result was that the bed left our quarters at once, and
we declared our intention of maintaining our ground.
How Dr. C—— could suppose that three in our
room was better than two in his I cannot imagine.

When the steamer came in which was to take my
late companions to Constantinople, I was lunching
with a friend, and therefore missed the farewell, for
which I consoled myself heroically. Hilton remained, together with the Philologist and his wife.
My last memory of Hilton was borrowing a shilling
of him, because I did not happen to have Turkish
money. While I was paying a visit he left suddenly
on the steamer for Egypt, and I saw him no more.
I still owe him that shilling. If these lines should
ever meet his eye, I beg he will communicate with
me, for that debt has weighed heavily all this time,
and I would fain have it discharged. I had learned
to know him well and to like him extremely, so
could not wish him to think I was like others he had
met.

The philolhgist and his wife returned with me,
and I bade farewell to them at Brindisi. I have so
much kindness to remember at their hands, both in
the East and afterward in London, that I must pay
the tribute due to the English character, which is
capable of such true, kindly, and disinterested
friendship.

Beirût is truly a beautiful city, but not very interesting to the sightseer. Antiquity does not accord

it much fame. In
fact, its glory is to
come. For, situ-
ated as it is, it
promises to be the
port of the great
country lying to
the east, when that
land shall have
once obtained just
rulers. Indeed, its
prosperity is daily increasing, and it is, perhaps, the
most thriving town on all this coast. The streets
are clean, fairly well built, and show evidences of
wealth and prosperity. Villas surround the town,
the walls have almost disappeared, and Beirût, instead of being the crumbling remains of past glory,
is taking on every day more beauty and more importance. The intensely blue sea spreads itself out
in front, making the mountains in the distance, as
they disappear toward the north, appear pale in
comparison.

The Syrians dress in their own costume, but are
neat and respectable, while men of all nationalities
throng its streets. Doubtless, the American Mission, established nearly seventy years ago, has done
much to educate its inhabitants and to attract the

foreign element. Large buildings, occupied by the schools, and neat, comfortable houses along the shore proclaim the Anglo-Saxon element. Far out on the promontory stands a stone house, built by native hands, but used now by the venerable mission- ary and revered scholar, Dr. Cor- nelius Van Dyck. Here, surrounded on two sides by the sea, with a view far out on the blue expanse, was writ-

ten many of those pages which have done more for Christianity than years of teaching. Here, away from the city, but in easy reach of it, is a home, half Arabic, half American. The house, adapted to the uses of the family, presents almost the appear- ance of luxury. The veranda surrounding it is covered with vines. The rocks below it are dashed by the waves. Even in the hottest days of summer a breeze sweeps over this point of land, so that there is little necessity for the family to move to the mountains when the hot season comes on. To Dr. Van Dyck I must return many thanks for his con- sideration and his great kindness.

Of the Mission I can only say that, outwardly, it

is most flourishing. While I have yet to see the mission I consider successful in point of fact, here one, perhaps, has as little reason to find fault as anywhere. It is, I think, an open secret that mission work has failed, so far as preaching is concerned. Now the attention is turned entirely toward teaching. That this is judicious is unquestionable. But the thought comes to one that teaching is not, and was not, the original design of missions. Therefore it is simply an excuse, a letting down from the original standard. The whole system must be judged by its results. Teaching, when it does not convert, is so much willful misapplication of people's funds. "We have in Beirût a splendid instance of the power of Christianity," I hear many people say. But I should say, "a splendid instance of the power of money." To-day there are a college, a medical school, and a preparatory department. There are numerous other schools scattered all throughout this region, one hundred and eighteen in all, with five thousand pupils. There are nearly twenty missionaries in the whole station, and perhaps fifteen or twenty teachers in the Beirût schools, not counting the natives employed. The president of the college gets two thousand dollars, the others in proportion. Let anyone estimate the expense, and add to this three hundred dollars a year for each native teacher, of whom there must be at least one hundred, and then put with it all the expenses of the college and the churches, beside expenses for apparatus, for bringing missionaries out, and so forth. As a result—a net result in figures—for the enthusiastic imagination of a returned missionary is hardly trustworthy, we have thirteen hundred communicants in the whole station, and not one self-supporting church. What does this mean? Add up all the hundreds of thousands of dollars, nay, millions, and divide it by thirteen hundred. The result is the expense per capita. Then reflect that these missions were sent to the Arabs, and have not converted a single Moslem, unless there be one alone on record. The converts come from the Latin and Greek churches; in other words, all this vast undertaking is simply for proselytism.

Religious papers are filled with glowing accounts of the success of missions, and of this one in particular. I have yet to read a statement, both positive and yet true, which shows a success. When figures are mentioned, missionaries turn away in scorn and say:

"Figures are not to be considered when the Lord's work is being done."

This may be true. But every giving man has a right to know where his money goes, and just what good it is doing. To keep him in ignorance or to blind him by glowing reports is what business men would look at as a very serious matter. As a last resort they say the mission has great influence, and is permeating the whole country. Where is the evidence? It is impossible to produce it. The mission at Beirût is hated on all sides, and, instead of exerting such a beneficial influence, is making Christianity odious by its own petty quarrels. It is not necessary to cite the last disgraceful squabble. It is enough to relate how a certain religious paper came out with the startling announcement of the great progress Christianity had made in the East. The article related that a certain gentleman in Beirût, who shall be nameless, had just finished his great work, the translation into Arabic of the leading Calvinistic writers. Calvinism for the Arabs ! I say no more ; I leave it to the thought of my readers.

And yet, I fancy, the majority of the missionaries are devoted men. Not, remember, men who are undergoing any very great hardships. Their lot is far better than that of many a poor missionary I could name within one hundred miles of New York. It is a mistaken notion that it is an awful undertaking to live in the East. A certain well-known family, after years spent there, will not live anywhere else. The whole point of the matter is, are we more responsible for the souls of the Moslems, who will not be converted, than we are for the wretched inhabitants of lower New York, or those of many of our larger cities ?

If common sense and business methods are out of place in Christian work, I, for one, cannot wonder at the present amount of skepticism.

But Beirût stands like a gem in the sea as I sail away, leaving far behind those lovely shores, whose mountains and vales linger like some pleasing dream in the memory. The gently-lapping sea murmurs softly, the peaks of Lebanon fade from sight ; rock, plain, and sand are gone, and all around is water, blue and beautiful, while the mind continues to gaze into the distance, as though seeking some point more, as a token or answering gleam to the beauties of the imagination—the fairest spot made by Nature's hand, the home of the artist, the center of a new and, we trust, a greater civilization than the present !